WHAT PRICE GLORY -- IN TRANSLATION?

Marilyn Gaddis Rose (SUNY/Binghamton)
Norman Simms (University of Waikato, N.Z.)
Elizabeth Welt Trahan (The Monterey Institute for International Studies)

ALSO IN THIS ISSUE:

ABSTRACTS (Review of National Literatures)
 ARMENIA

CNL: A "RETROSPECTIVE" (1974–1984)

PUBLISHED BY "GRIFFON HOUSE" FOR

COUNCIL on NATIONAL LITERATURES

P.O. BOX 81 • WHITESTONE, NEW YORK 11357

A Forum for scholars concerned with comparative study of the established, emergent, and neglected national literatures that make up the written and oral artistic legacy of the diverse contemporary peoples of the world.

PN
24/
N52
1987

Contents

INTRODUCTION

This issue—the first in the new annual *CNL/WORLD REPORT*—will provide an expanded outlet for the important "continuing dialogue" between comparatists and special area experts in emergent and neglected (especially "non"-Western) literatures. *CNL/WR* will serve as an essential companion volume to *REVIEW OF NATIONAL LITERATURES*, in which model "overviews" of literatures not in the European mainstream are provided in an organic and representative format. Eventually, the Editors hope to launch a third series which will provide much-needed translations (in a modest publishing program) for use in experimental projects throughout the country in "multinational" comparative literary studies.

The present volume contains excellent discussions on translation and classroom experiments with non-Western literatures; it also provides the Abstracts for the *RNL* volume on *Armenia*—one of the most important recent publications in the *RNL* series.

This first volume of *CNL/WR* also contains a "retrospective" —the first 10 years (1974-1984) of the Council on National Literatures: an assessment which includes some early milestones, such as the special presentation to Professor James G. McManaway on the occasion of the publication of the *Shakespeare and England* volume of *RNL*; a major bilingual program on Shakespeare; a 10th-anniversary awards-dinner in Washington D.C.; a special reception/presentation ceremony at The New York Public Library on the occasion of the publication of the *Armenia* volume of *RNL;* and a review of CNL activities to-date and plans for the future.

The Editors and Board of Directors take great pride in announcing this first issue in the newly-expanded *CNL/WR* series. Members are urged to renew their dues and to insure the continued success of this unique and growing world-wide organization (in over forty foreign countries).

CNL is a nonprofit educational foundation. It is self-sufficient, financed by membership dues and occasional grants and gifts. All dues and donations are tax-deductible.

CONSOLIDATION AND CONSENSUS:
CONTENTION AND CONGRUENCE

Marilyn Gaddis Rose
(SUNY Binghamton)

The decade 1974-1984 was radically, albeit quietly, revolutionary in translation studies. Looking back, we see the formation of a mainstream which has in no way abated and which may be expected to enlarge its channel. Within it are several strong currents which unpredictably, but productively, merge and separate. The first is consolidation, that is, the organization of translation groups, chiefly in the Northern hemisphere but increasingly including the Southern Hemisphere as well, into an interlocking network. The second is consensus which is both cause and result of the consolidation. The third is contention, for within the consolidation there are ideological eddies competing for domination of the mainstream. The fourth is congruence, the parallel directions and velocities which, despite the ripples on the surface, can be discerned by an observer on the bridge.

Let me take up consolidation first, the coordination of activities among organizations. The Federation international des traducteurs (FIT) was founded in Paris in 1955 under UNESCO sponsorship, but not, however, as a UNESCO agency. It began its networking first with established national organizations like the British Translators Guild and the American Translators Association (ATA). And there the matter rested until August, 1976 when at the International Comparative Literature Association (ICLA) Congress in Budapest, FIT sent representatives for a joint meeting with the ICLA Translation Studies Committee. This relationship has continued with each group being represented at the other's congresses. Inasmuch as FIT is affiliated in the same way with the Association internationale de la linguistique appliquee (AILA), comparatist translation scholars interact with both professional translators and linguists. On the current elected ICLA translation Studies Committee, there are representatives from AILA and FIT. We American comparatists, in turn, have had a role both in bringing international concerns to American organizations and in taking to the international organizations the Humanist (and comparatist) perspectives of the American comparative curriculum. To be specific: at the premiere American Literary Translatiors Association (ALTA) meeting in Dallas, in 1978, organized by Rainer Schulte and Leslie Wilson, those present amended the draft constitution to include translation theory in its purview. In 1980, the leadership of ATA recognized that it had been remiss in this area and inaugurated a plenary session, "Translating Translation Theory," at its San Francisco meeting in August. In 1982 incoming ATA President Ben Teague created a standing committee in Translation Studies. ATA is the American FIT affiliate, but because of the networking and overlap, the ATA delegation to the 1984 FIT Congress included an ALTA member (a comparatist) with other ALTA comparatists taking part in the open sessions and standing committees. The de facto circle is now complete, a completely interlocking network; to stay with my original conceit, a dragnet.

The network would not have come into existence if its time had not come, and now we come to consensus. In terms of language cycles, world society is now living through two conflicting language impulses. First, we are in an upcurve of the cycle of ethnic linguistic nationalism; groups which have, as far as most of us knew, been using their country's dominant language for 200 or 300 years, are in another period of resurgence. Their determination to use their own language sometimes takes violent forms. The Wycliffe Bible Society anthropologists tally the world's languages at 5,200, a figure large enough to cause panic. But at the same time, to return to the second impulse, there is widespread recognition that one must use a major world language, if not natively, additionally. (Arabic, Chinese, English, Russian, Spanish, in terms of native user base; French, German, and Japanese also if we consider official and commercial language status.) French and English are the official languages of both FIT and ICLA. Thus, translators and researchers in support disciplines (anthropology, linguistics, pedagogy, philosophy, psychology, etc.) and user disciplines (economics, engineering, history, management, political science, etc.) see the role of translation as critical, if not desperate. Translators themselves see this, and they, their governments, and their international agencies are aware that research and experimentation, amplification and improvement of practice are urgent and call for coordination. Since research which retrieves, expands, and advances knowledge is never frivolous, literary scholars and historians, lexicographers and terminologists, critics and analysts are welcomed. The contention is not between pure and applied linguistics, not between technology and literature.

Rather the contention, especially the contentiousness, comes within the nature of the tentative conclusions, the dogmatism of expression and argument, the competition of leaders for followers. For this move to study translation, in many respects the move to use aesthetic experience as data, calling literature a form of production and calling the literature classroom a laboratory, has been seen throughout the world, in both free and planned economies. While translation studies was valorizing theory over practice, translation theory was becoming a boundary discipline between Comparative Literature and many other areas. Further, since translation is the comparatist's essential tool for dealing with cultures besides his or her own, it has been difficult for any comparatist to escape this tendency. Indeed, since Comparative Literature has valorized literary theory over literature, translation studies has profited as much as any branch of Comparative Literature from this tendency. Comparatists in translation studies even had an advantage over their other comparatist colleagues, for translation studies was already using the ideas and data from linguistics; translation studies already knew the vocabularies of the various disciplines which contribute to linguistics. Its practitioners had already been studying the process and product of translating and were in a position to move into such a study of criticizing and reading. We have seen it happen, and it was predictable. The methods of translation studies, gathered from the support disciplines already mentioned, served for Comparative Literature and vice versa. (I am thinking of Even-Zohar, Holmes, Lambert, Lefevere, Rose, Toury; Bjornson, Caws, DeMan, Derrida, Mitchell, Vázquez-Ayora.) Prior to 1974, we might have had to explain to English department colleagues on all-school curriculum committees that translation was a critical tool. After 1974, no one questioned the validity of the tool. The number of dissertations involving translation, theoretical or conceptual with the personal practical experiment, i.e., the translation, show that the procedure has been accepted.

Indeed, George Steiner's *After Babel* (1975) brought the procedure and related issues to the general reader. But not many people actually engaged in the field accepted his division into Chomsky and Whorf camps. After all, even when the translation scholars are all comparatists as is the case with the dozen or so I have mentioned thus far, we have not all had the same training or come from the same traditions. We do not have the same concepts or conjectures. At worst we have what Andre Lefevere has called "semantic terrorism," at best a plethora of near-synonyms. Some people in the field are persuaded that they have channeled the main form of the mainstream. (They have probably just renamed the ripples.) And some colleagues have different forces impelling them to a certain current. Sometimes it would seem that East Europeans must conceal their love of literature behind a screen of research, looking for the norms and the social forces determining them. Some West Europeans and Americans, it would seem, conceal their boredom with literature the same way. Just as entirely too many comparatists have not read anything except literary criticism for a decade, too many translation analysts keep going through translations of established texts, rather than translating themselves. The observer on the bridge could easily find research teams in, say, both Belgium and Czechoslovakia engaged in building models of the translation process or counting the use of, say, "de" prepositional phrases replacing English qualitative adjectives, i.e., the transformation of "floral bouquet" into "bouquet de fleurs" in French translations of *The Vicar of Wakefield* between 1767 and 1860. One group, free to research anything, is strangely evasive about liking what they have read; the other group, restricted to canonical texts, preferably those written before 1917, are also strangely evasive about what they have read. But both teams are collating data on literary history, cycles of artistic changes, the role of the literary producer, the critic, the types of freedom and restraint operative in their milieu.

Meanwhile, concurrently, and usually unilaterally, merging disciplines which also border on Comparative Literature and which enlist the attention of many comparatist translators use such data and contribute their own. The international nature of literary knowledge requires going among languages and that means encountering difference. I use the word advisedly since Derrida began spelling "difference" with an "a" after comparing Hegel in German with a French translation. And the translation, even if "wrong" in a sense, may have made an independent contribution to culture and, hence, literature. Consider the famous example of Freud as translated by James Strachey; Bruno Bettelheim would have us believe that generations of psychoanalysts have been misled by the translator's choice of "Id," "Ego," and "Superego," but these terms, not their homey literal counterparts, have acquired authority. Any such incursion into language and usage is bound to have meaningful repercussions on knowledge generally, certainly on a discipline as intent upon criticism and theory as Comparative Literature. And in every instance, translation, usually in the narrowest definition, is at the crux of the matter.

But the key here is "concurrently," for unpleasant as a coterie conference can occasionally be when one is the token representative of a camp perceived as opposing, the differences lie, in my opinion, more with the personalities contending than with the discipline providing a forum for the contention. To return to my opening conceit, the 1984 FIT Congress was awash with cooperation. (When the American delegation put forward bylaws to make the organization more democratic, the Russian delegation came in with a friendly emendation, making unanimity possible; the meetings of the standing committees were just as cordial and constructive.) All these efforts go toward understanding expression and appreciating it. Americans generally are eclectic, neutralizing their ideological opposition by selective amalgamation. (I am thinking here of Eugene Nida, sociolinguist who established modern translation studies with a publication in 1945.) The British prune away terminology and try to make subtle notions sound like ordinary common sense. (I am thinking here of Nida's British counterpart Peter Newmark.) The Germans are prone to build sophisticated models (consider Wolfram Wilss and Katarina Reiss) which the East Europeans develop to the final flourish (consider those of the late Anton Popovič), the French express their theories as genial provocations (Danica Seleskovitch would claim "les mots disparaîssent"), while the polystream proponents (primarily Israelis and the Belgians who borrowed from them) call themselves a "mafia" and try to overwhelm both their antagonists and the bystanders (Even-Zohar and Toury, Lefevere and Lambert). But amidst the occasional babel there is a comforting realization. Translators and translation theorists, whether lovers or loathers of literature, have all been reading it. Even the graduate students poring over successive French translations of *The Vicar of Wakefield* have been reading it word for word. Even if *malgré eux*, they have had an aesthetic experience, they have taken an 18th-century English pastoral into their lives. Those inhibited from creating literature have been allowed to read it through translation or translation studies.

Eventually, and thankfully, literary theory and criticism, even when diverted through the most mechanical of exercises in translation research, even when channeled between the banks of *The Vicar of Wakefield*, gets us back to literature. And that, after all, is the ultimate source of the translation studies mainstream.

WORKS CITED

Bettelheim, Bruno, "Freud and the Soul," *The New Yorker*, March 1, 1982, pp. 52-93.
Derrida, Jacques, *Marges*. Paris: Minuit, 1972.
Lefevere, André, co-editor, *The Art and Science of Translation*, monograph issue of *Dispositio*, 7 (1982). This gives a sampling of all polysystematizers and some of their opponents.
Newmark, Peter, *Approaches to Translation*. Oxford: Pergamon, 1981.

Nida, Eugene, "Linguistics and Ethnology in Translation Problems," *Word*, 1 (1945), pp. 194-208.

---------------------- and Charles R. Taber, *The Theory and Practice of Translation*. Leiden: E. J. Brill, 1974.

Popovič, Anton, *Translation in the Literary Process*. Nitra: Pedagogickej Faculty, 1982.

Reiss, Katarina, *Texttyp und Ubersetzungsmethode*. Kronberg/Ts.: Scriptor Verlag, 1976.

Seleskovitch, Danica, *Interpreting for International Conferences*. Trans. Stephanie Dailey and E. N. McMillan. Washington D.C.: Pen and Booth, 1978.

Steiner, George, *After Babel*. New York: Oxford, 1975.

Wilss, Wolfram, *The Science of Translation*. Philadelphia: John Benjamins, 1982.

ON THE FRINGES: TRANSLATION AND PSEUDO-TRANSLATION IN INTERCULTURAL ENCOUNTERS

Norman Simms
(University of Waikato, N.Z.)

For the purposes of this paper, I am going to lift the process and the concept of translation from the silent and invisible zone of the professional writer's study (where one lone figure, hunched over a text, surrounded by dictionaries, moves the thoughts, feelings, and images of one piece of literary writing into the text of another language), and I am going to place it out in the world, into a geographical space in which two sets of people, unequally related by numbers, military arms, and knowledge of the situation, confront each other across two distinct languages, and where control over the language of the other both is a product of and produces the unequal meeting. In the first zone, the familiar interior region of literary translation, what is important is the validity of the translation process itself, as well as the integrity of the new text in relationship to a past original creative act and to the resonances of the target language. In this private situation, with rare exceptions, it is the translator who approaches with humility the text to be translated and learns respect by the strategies and finesse used to render it into another language. It may well be that the translation exceeds the original, as the French version of Poe surpasses the original. More usually the translation leads a tentative life of dependence upon the original, almost of necessity replaced by subsequent and repeated acts of translation as it succeeds in arousing interest in the literature revealed to the target language.

In the second external space, however, the languages confront one another in hostility, suspicion, and apprehension, each language fixed not in a distinct text but dispersed amongst particular individuals and groups, each trying to control the encounter itself. While to a certain extent each set of individuals and groups perceives the other initially as the object of a translation act, the dynamics of the encounter soon begin to designate one or the other as the target language, effectively as the subject of the translation. This may happen moreover in a number of ways, either with the dominant group forcing the other to speak in the language of the superior force, in a third lingua franca they designate, or in their own tongue; in this last case, the superior group thus expresses its mastery over the inferior language and refuses to accept the ability or capabilities of the other to make a translation at all.

The process and concept of translation thus widened to the outside world needs to be seen as something other than the interior of silent and invisible background to the text of some other language we see before us as a work of introduced literature. The external process we are looking at bristles with hostile power-relations and the concept of translation is riddled with attempts to do many things other than render an integral version of the original text: there are attempts to use deception, ruse, and other tricks in order to protect the speaker and his or her party, to hold back or deflect the power of the other language group, to enhance one's own position and denigrate the other, to flatter, mislead, cajole, and so forth. In other words, translation becomes an instrument of intense manipulation of the power and play on the knowledge inherent in language.

The two examples I wish to examine are somewhat disappointing in terms of displaying any actual in-the-field encounter between opposing civilizations, such as Tzvetan Todorov examines in his *Conquest of America.*[1] For my two examples come from early English novels and they only pretend to be descriptions of situations in which separate language groups meet in the field of translation. Examination of them will, however, offer insight into the kind of bristling confrontation between different mentalities that is characteristic of the encounter between a superior and an inferior social organization speaking different languages, and at the same time point towards a way in which we should address the origins of the novel itself. Following Mikhail Bakhtin[2] and Lennard J. Davis,[3] we must look for the clash of social discourses against the hegemonic authority of literary genres. I will thus be suggesting rather strongly that the act and concept of translation can involve transferences of knowledge and power (relations) within a distinct national language, and that the possibility of this kind of transformation—or even of a revolution—depends not only on changing conditions within the boundaries of the language zone itself but also on the reality of encounters between that language and distinctly different others at its peripheries. This is partly because the perception of the revolutionary changes in the national (metropolitan) society cannot be focused within the generic givens of the official literary discourses and so must be imagined, projected out to the regions of exotic confrontation, i.e., those which were previously unseen and heard by the society in the process of internal change even when the impetus for that change derives in great measure from the discovery of those distant and unthinkable regions of the world. It is also because, as the genres themselves and the discourses they contain weaken under the actual transformations, a new modality of speech and narration, the novel, registers its control over the national language by taking it into these imaginary encounters with the other and showing through its translation its superiority. If we ask then, "What price glory is translation?" we would have to answer, in this set of instances, that the movement of the new middle classes and of women into serious public discourses of literature is paid for by the denigration of the other, of American Indian languages, the reduction of their speech into barbarism, and their knowledge systems into savagery and superstition.

Now let me begin by outlining my two specimen texts. The first I will examine, though the second to be actually written, is a passage from the sequel to Daniel Defoe's *Life and Adventures of Robinson Crusoe* known as *The Further Adventures.*[4] It is an episode reported to Crusoe on his return to his island off the coast of Brazil by his colonists. The Spaniards, who are the most civilized and respectable, tell him of an adventure undertaken by the more uncouth English sailors; they paddled out in search of Indians to capture as slaves to do the work they were too lazy to do for themselves. The second example, written earlier, comes from Mrs. Aphra Behn's novel *Oroonoko,*[5] a narrative blending autobiographical details of her stay in Surinam as a young woman and the romantic tragedy of the noble African hero whose name gives the book its title. Moving into the foreground of action, the female narrator of *Oroonoko* recounts her journey inland from the coast to meet with a tribe of Indians who had never before seen Europeans. Thus, in Defoe's case, the example is deliberately distanced from the reader by a series of textual layers of discourse: we are reading what Daniel Defoe writes in the person of Robinson Crusoe who has heard it from the Spaniards who report what the English sailors have told them. In Aphra Behn's novel, however, the key incident seems almost to break the decorum of the narrative fiction and to appear as a personal revelation by the author. Yet both novels turn on the problematic of an imagined translation.

The Spanish citizens of Robinson Crusoe's island report to him the account of the story they have learned from the three unruly Englishmen who went out in search of slaves to ease their lazy lives. The sailors take a canoe to another island, come across sociable and apparently friendly Indians, who explain to them by sign language that they have two hundred prisoners of war they are saving for a cannibal feast. "The Englishmen," we overhear the Spaniards telling Crusoe indirectly, "seemed mighty desirous to see those prisoners: but the others mistaking them, thought they were desirous to have some of them, to carry away for their own eating." Thus, the first problem of mistranslation arises when the Indians assume that the Englishmen are, like themselves, anthropophages.[6] Communication is limited by a reduced verbal capacity on both sides and the inherent ambiguities of informal hand signs, but also greatly interfered with by the differences in mentalities between the two nationalities. The situation is further complicated by what the Spanish interlocutors report to Crusoe. "As brutish as these fellows [i.e., the Englishmen] were at home, their stomachs turned at this sight . . . ." Up to this point, so far as Crusoe and his respectable citizens are concerned, the sailors are nasty brutes, but separated from the surrounding "savages," the Indians, by the wearing of clothing and the carrying of arms (guns). Here an essential qualifying distinction is opened: the others, the real savages, eat human flesh, while "christians," no matter of what particular European nation, have no stomach for such a custom.[7] The outward signs of brutishness in the Englishmen, which is recognized in relative terms by the Spaniards within the mentality of European civilization as a degraded form of Christian behavior, are misread by the Indians as indicative of a similar enthusiasm for cannibal food. The Indians, then, are being read not merely as normally in the state of degradation which these English Europeans have fallen into, but much worse; their norm is unrestrained by Christian morality which holds the sailors back from a final plunge into savagery.

When the prisoners are brought to the Englishmen, the sailors realize there is no way they can refuse the gift without insulting their hosts and thereby endangering their own lives. Interestingly, in telling this to Crusoe the Spaniards say—or, since the speech is indirect, and we are hearing this through Crusoe's own voice, it may be that Crusoe says—"to refuse prisoners would have been the highest affront to the savage gentry." This phrase casts the whole discourse of narration into a level of mock formality and dignity clearly not intrinsic to the fictional encounter. We have to see, therefore, that the discomfort of the Englishmen, as well as the misreadings of the savages, is an object of entertainment to the Spaniards, to Crusoe, and presumably to us as subsequent readers. This, of course, will be considered later, when we come to assess the doubling-back of the text upon itself in the course of its intellectual history. For the moment, we need only consider the difficulty of the Englishmen and the reportage of the Spaniards.

After giving the Indians a few trinkets which they fail to understand as "payment" or "reciprocity" in return for the five women and eleven men prisoners, but which the savages "seemed extremely pleased with," the Englishmen realize that they must leave at once, otherwise they would be expected to begin the cannibal feast that evening. Though the sailors are clearly disturbed by the situation that they have mistakenly brought on themselves in failing to communicate their precise wish for slaves and not for flesh on the hoof, as it were, the perspective of the Spaniards—and outwards through Crusoe to the reader—favors the Europeans. Like the reader, they understand more than the Indians: they both know what they failed to communicate and what they have unwittingly signaled. The advantage is surely theirs, since they can maneuver behind appearances to escape, while the Indians can only see in the Europeans what they are allowed to see by the limitations of their language and mentality. They are not objects of their own interpretation of the event.

Given that, the superiority of the textual perspective reduced the Englishmen and the Indians, so that we are told: "But having taken their leave, with all the respect and thanks that could well pass between people, where, on either side, they understood not one word they could say, they put off with their boat . . . ." This reading perspective equalizes the brutish sailors and the "savage gentry" to idiots, people who have no language between them. It belongs to the Spaniards, to Crusoe, and to the book—hence, to us.

Yet once the sailors are alone with their prisoners the situation at once reverts to a paradigm of European superiority over the savage, and opens to a more complex view of the Indians, with unstated implications to the frame narratives and, eventually, to our own modern reading of the text.

For when they are alone with the Indians, the Englishmen try to speak to their prisoners. It is not a dialogue they seek but a posture of authority: "but it was impossible to make them understand any thing . . . ." This seems, at first, to redound against the sailors, too, insofar as they are foolish in attempting to address the Indians when they clearly should recognize the lack of ability to translate on either side. It is as though they expected their current strategic advantage to force the others to comprehend. Yet "nothing they could say to them, or give them, or do for them, but was looked upon as going about to murder them . . . they immediately concluded they were unbound on purpose to be killed." It is, of course, a matter of cultural expectations: the Indian prisoners can neither think nor imagine that the strangers wish to do anything other than other Indians would do, kill and eat them. Even after the Indians recognize a certain kindness in the Englishmen's behavior, "still they expected every day to make a dinner or supper for their new masters." The situation seems to be at a stalemate. The Indians are painted with no mental equipment to see beyond the normative values of their own society, to understand, decode, or make sense of the different actions of the Englishmen; and the sailors, brutish specimens of European civilization as they are, have no way to communicate their real purposes to the remaining prisoners, eight of the men having been left on a nearby island as too much for them to handle.

At that point in Defoe's text, when the "wonderful history, or journal" of the English sailors is completed, and when the Spaniards turn to report to Crusoe what they themselves have seen and experienced, the situation begins to shift. For after returning to Crusoe's island, the sailors come to beg food from the Spaniards. The Spaniards, two other more civilized Englishmen, and Friday's father go to view the slaves that have been brought back, and they find them naked and bound in a hut on the other side of the island. At once, the previously undifferentiated mass of dumb (non-speaking) savages begins to resolve into distinct, that is, different speaking individuals, first by being described according to age and appearance, with recognition of their specific "shape and features." Moreover, the response of the Spaniards to this "uncouth" sight is objectified by Robinson Crusoe who assures the readers of their sensitivity and hence their civilized (literate) disgust at the way in which the Indians—especially the immodest manner in which the women—were treated. Because they are more cultured, we are implicitly told, the Spaniards can perceive the Indians in a way very different from that of the English sailors; they can receive more varied details and articulate them. The civilized readers of the scene have a wider vocabulary, and already, being Spaniards who communicate in English, see and feel more about the Indians than the sailors, give to them a larger semantic and semiotic zone in which to inhabit. At the same time, we also sense a much greater involvement of Crusoe's own sensibility in the descriptions of the text, such as when we are told that, of the women, "two of them had they been perfect white, would have passed for handsome women, even in London itself . . . especially when they came backwards to be clothed . . . ."

Having thus seen the Indians and, in doing so, granting to them more of a mental space in which to emerge as differentiated human beings, the Spaniards then call upon Friday's father to view them, to find out whether he recognizes any of them, and finally to test whether he understands their language. Here we have the tamed savage, as it were, or at least a member of the other mentality who has already, like his more famous son, submerged his own essential savage being within the authoritative identity of the European, mediating for them with the ignorant others and serving them to a point of near idolatry. He has become a projection of the European's superior control over the language situation and is effectively an instrument of their domination. He is their translator—he is their translation. Friday's father does not recognize any of the slaves and finds only one among them, a woman, with whom he can communicate.

The single Indian woman,[8] then, acts as an interpreter to the rest, "for it seems they were of several nations." When the information can be communicated that the Europeans are Christians, civilized, and unwilling to eat them and want them only as servants, "they all fell a dancing" and to make signs that they were indeed willing to work. A great deal is unsaid here, the burden of the narrative falling on the derogatory and derisive view of the ignorant savages pleased to be slaves instead of meals. We should, however, ask questions of the text, such as why it is a woman who can mediate between Friday's father and the other Indians, what lingua franca they use between their nations, and how they understand, if at all, the notion that their captors are "christians."

It is only after these basic matters are settled and the narrative turns to the subject of distributing the female slaves among the English sailors as concubines or, finally, as wives, that we move a further step inwards from the ironic modalities of generic paraphrase and indirect literary discourse to several phrases of direct speech, that is, begin to touch the fictional reality itself, the novel. Interestingly and tellingly, it is the Spanish governor who is given his own full sentence, while the others are given an undifferentiated though quotation-marked "no" to speak. It is because that civilized Spaniard's voice can be equivalent to Robinson Crusoe's own civilized textual voice that we then close the circle, and confirm that voice in the supplemental events of this episode. First, there is the account of how the worst and most brutish of the English sailors are tamed by their Indian wives; and second, how later, a real marriage is arranged for them by a French priest Crusoe had picked up from a shipwreck en route to his island. The institution of marriage and its sacramental enhancement conclude the taming both of the Indian movement of communication that goes from the sensitive differentiating descriptions of the Spanish citizens through Friday's father to the woman mediator and thence to the other savages. That concatenation is enmeshed in and surrounded by the textualizing presence of the novel's narrator. As surrogate for Crusoe, the governor may speak in his own voice, since it is, in fine, the same as the narrator's. At that point, further, the civilization of Spain, all its brutalities in conquest of the New World notwithstanding nor its Catholic superstitions, merges with the pragmatic and rational civilization of England, its own lawless ruffians and hooligans taken into consideration.

Yet intrinsic to the text itself, deep in its novelistic tensions between the spoken and the unspoken, there are problematics we need to address. For these raise the question of translation up from the comic encounter between the three sailors and a tribe of savage Indians. They ask us, at the same time, and perhaps even more incisively, to consider the translations of experience from the words and actions of real or fictional events through the generic categories of literate textuality (as in rhetoric) to the new textuality of the novel. We shall come back to this point again after we examine the next specimen text, the passage from Aphra Behn's *Oroonoko: or, The Royal Slave.*

Mrs. Behn's narrative, which is now recognized as one of the key turning points in the development of the novel,[9] is an apparent mixing of two tales, the one giving the romantic (romance) story of a royal African slave transported to the New World, and the other a first person narrative of a woman's adventures in Surinam, a tale increasingly recognized as based on the actual experiences of young Aphra Behn herself.[10] The problematic of the novel's textual presence as a fiction will be discussed later. For the moment, we wish to look at a particular event described by the narrator in which she rather than Oroonoko is simultaneously subject and object of the discourse.

At a time when the local Indians are beginning to fall upon the English coastal settlements in Surinam, Aphra's unnamed female narrator thinks of a long cherished wish to visit the Indians of the interior, a visit made possible further by Oroonoko's promise of protection. The object of the visit is to observe a group of Indians in their first encounter with Europeans. This has recently been noticed by feminist critics as significant as an act of female independence and daring by Mrs. Behn,[11] but nothing further of the implications has been explored. I would like to suggest that the incident encapsulates a tight knot of unspeakable and unimaginable qualities about the mentality of England in the last third of the seventeenth century, and that the immediate question of translation is to be held under erasure for a set of much more unthinkable questions.

As the party of women and their attendant males prepare to move into the jungles of Guyana, Mrs. Behn's narrator remarks:

> Now, none of us speaking the language of the people, and imagining we should have a half diversion in gazing only; and not knowing what they said, we took a fisherman that liv'd at the mouth of the river, who had been a long inhabitant there, and oblig'd him to go with us: But because he was

known to the *Indians*, as trading among 'em and being by long living there, became a perfect *Indian* in colour, we who had a mind to surprize 'em by making them see something they had never seen (that is *White* people) resolv'd only my self, my brother and woman should go: so *Caesar* [i.e. Oroonoko under his slave name], the fisherman and the rest hiding behind some thick reeds and flowers that grew in the banks, let us pass on towards the town, which was on the bank of the river all along. (pp. 200-201)

The expectation is that the diversion will be incomplete since the narrator and the other women cannot understand the language of the Indians. They will only "gaze" at the "surprise" of the savages viewing white people. The woman wishes to make herself seem an object, a strange thing, for the Indians to stare at; while she actually, silently within her mind, gazes out at them, with a superior sense of her own presence, an ability not only to see them but also to imagine herself in the midst of their expected savage antics of surprise. The fisherman who knows their language and by long exposure to the elements and the environment has become an Indian in appearance stands by, deferred as a translator if necessary to protect the narrator, just as Oroonoko himself hides behind the riverbank but is close enough to rescue her from any immanent danger. Thus much more than the brute English sailors in Defoe's account, where the superiority of the gaze comes in the subsequent textualization of the Spaniards and Crusoe himself, as they regard the encounter between the Indians and the sailors, here it is directly in the fiction that the critical gaze operates. Though the inability to understand the Indian language partly mitigates the "diversion" of the game, it is willingly held in suspension, since the fisherman is close by and specifically asked to hide from view until the moment of originary encounter can be executed. That the fisherman, who has only taken on the appearance of an Indian in color and linguistic skill, already "was known to" them does not enter into the calculations: a white woman, the narrator, will surprise them entirely.

The small party then approaches the Indian village. The inhabitants are dancing and, when they spy the white people, they began to cry in a loud voice and gather around the narrator. She is frightened, yet continues, only later reassuring herself that they were not threatening noises but signs of "wonder and amazement." Then the narrator describes the Indians and herself in relation to them in a lengthy passage in which she attempts to imagine herself and her brother as though from the eyes of the Indians, to construct what they are saying and thinking, despite the lack of language between them.

The Indians are trying to read by touching the signs of the strangers, the icons, that have come into their midst. The narrator and her woman particularly allow the Indian men to feel them and gaze at them in a way which is sexual, to say the least. There is already to hand the traveler's vocabulary of virgin land, penetration by conquerors, rape of the landscape, and so on. What is remarkable, then, is that the female narrator allows her own body and that of her waiting woman to be treated in the very way in which European voyagers and explorers have treated the body of the New World.

What the narrator does here and elsewhere in the account is to re-enact, in miniature, what the British and Spanish conquerors have done to the Indians, abusing their intellectual prowess (as much through technological skills as through the reflexivity of their conceptualizations of the encounters) and crushed the delicate flower of these lesser folk. But the actual text of the fictional encounter, seen *in extenso*, does not allow for this conclusion to rest easily.

Where later at the turn of the century Defoe creates a scenario of European and Indian meeting, he separates two kinds of superior beings: the crude English sailors who, while superior to the Indians only in their disgust at the idea of cannibalism, become more polished in association with the Indians through the mutually imposed institution of marriage; and the Spanish citizens of Crusoe's island, who, despite their Catholicism, nevertheless share in the intellectual and social refinements of general West European culture along with Crusoe himself, and through him, with Daniel Defoe. A chain of command, from Crusoe to Friday to Friday's father, leads to the single Indian translator, and then out from her to the other captive savages. For Defoe, then, it is the good old obedient native and the intelligent woman who mediate not only between Europeans and Indian society, who act as translators between these radically distinct mentalities, but also who permit a restoration of the fallen brutes, the English sailors, to a more socially acceptable position within the transplanted European society of Crusoe's island.

Hence, for all the radical-seeming re-assessments of the disposition between Old and New World cultures, Defoe's vision does not permit any significant realignment of the inner structures of the European civilization itself. On the other hand, Aphra Behn's vision is more subversive. She is more radical in her deconstruction of the European text, although the figure she puts forward of her narrator is ambiguous in its inability actually to save Oroonoko's life, since the suite of texts woven together to form the novel allows for a vision of a society in which women are active and intelligent forces for the good. The way in which this is accomplished, of course, depends on our willingness as readers to see more and other than the text claims to be saying and showing; it requires that we reconstitute the text according to the signals of its silences and invisibilities.

Just as the real communications between Indian and European are hindered by the lack of a common language but created through the good offices of the heroic black man: so the lapses, contradictions, non sequiturs of the text, standing between the reader and the narrator, the breaks in communication between, we should really say, the male-dominated generic discourses and the experiental reality of the world lived in by women (as well as men), comes through recognition of the displacements and supplementations of presence between Oroonoko and the narrator.

The text then, reveals a complexity of development which the voice of the narrator herself does not articulate clearly and explicitly. Counter to a discourse of digression, with its supposedly diversionary game and its more rhetorically purposeful depiction of Oroonoko's heroic character, there is another discourse, a discourse of anthropological gaze cast as much in the way of the European as of the Indian participants in the occasion. Moreover, just as the narrator claims that many of the events occuring on the journey back were "worthy reciting" although not given, so we can register another more silent discourse, evident by its traces, of the assertion of female integrity and determination; the presence of the text itself and its female narrator and female author manifest this discourse.

Our conclusion to this paper rests on four points of reading the text and its contexts. We have noted that Mrs. Behn, like other proto-feminists of the seventeenth century, sees in the black slaves of America outward figures of their own plight in England. Angeline Goreau cites two women authors to this effect: first, an anonymous writer in 1696 states quite explicitly that "Women, like our Negroes in our western plantations, are born slaves, and live prisoners all their lives"; and second, Mary Astell, writing in 1706, who asks, "If all men are born free, how is it that all women are born slaves?"[12] Goreau is, however, quite open in her indication of the relationship deeply embedded in Aphra Behn's text which inter-relates Oroonoko to the unnamed narrator (and note too how a black slave like Oroonoko has two names, his African title and his imposed slave-name, Caesar, while the female writer has none) in terms of the manipulation of knowledge. For the means by which Oroonoko is lured aboard the slave ship, when he is in his romantic glory as prince of the Gold Coast, is his intellectual curiosity.[13]

In that light, we argue, the narrator's adventure amongst the Indians is not merely an episode displaying "her courage and curiosity," but an ambiguous, even an equivocational event, virtually an impasse in the text: a moment when she is caught out displaying herself as proper women never must—that is, making herself into a sexual object, gaining a reputation (which is as much a negative sexual role as a misgotten masculine fame for intellectual prowess). She is, by this means, moreover, deconstructing the very texts she articulates: the narrative of European conquest over savage races, the romance of woman as icon of beauty to be adored, the pornographic exploration of sexual taboos, the as yet unwritten novel of women's equal place in European society.

But this doubling back of the displaced disgression in Mrs. Behn's novel needs to be seen in relation to Defoe's first continuation of *Robinson Crusoe*, so that the game of observing a fictional translation process permits the writing out of words and images otherwise still unspeakable and unthinkable in literary genres. The novel as the text of heteroglossia, as Bakhtin makes us aware, necessarily allows the breakthrough of unseen and unheard facets of human experience. At first, however, when the normally controlling boundaries of satire and farce are removed, this release requires the presence of a controlling narrative authority, a voice of reflective masculine authority, or at least, as in Mrs. Behn's case, a humble and apologetic woman.

The pseudo-translation of both novels signals the grounds of the textual revolution occuring. It happens in the breakdown of normative, traditional, rhetorical modalities of speech and knowledge. Just as it really was happening over a long period on the peripheries of Europe, in the sustained encounter between European knowledge and the cultures of the New Worlds opened up in America and the rest of the world, so it could happen in narratives only in fictionalized encounters at the fringes of society, sometimes projected outward to America or Africa, sometimes disclosed in taboo areas of Europe—in prisons and brothels, in the intimacy of the long-unspoken experiences of private experience. The fictionalized translation is, then, not a mere gambit, a pretence of being recorded in a language other than English, but a real translation, a shift within English itself from rhetorical and generic forms of discourse and address to the heteroglossia of the novel, of modern realities.

NOTES

1. Tzeveten Todorov, *The Conquest of America: The Question of the Other*. Trans. from French by Richard Howard. New York:

Harper & Row, 1984; orig. ed. 1982; See especially pp. 80, 97, and 159.

2. I have based much of this paper on the insights of the four essays collected in Mikhail M. Bakhtin, *The Dialogic Imagination*, trans. from Russian by Caryl Emersen and Michael Holquist, and ed. by Michael Holquist. Austin and London: University of Texas Press, 1981; University of Texas Press Slavic Series, No. 1.

3. Lennard J. Davis, "A Social History of Fact and Fiction: Authorrial Disavowal in the Early English Novel," in Edward W. Said, ed. *Literature and Society: Selected Papers from the English Institute, 1978*. New Series no.3. Baltimore and London: The John's Hopkins University Press, 1980, pp. 120-148.

4. I am using the 1865 edition, *The Life and Surprising Adventures of Robinson Crusoe: including an Account of his Long Residence on an Uninhabited Island; and many other Remarkable Incidents in his History*. Halifax: Milner and Soucby, 1965. See especially pp. 260-265 and 327-328.

5. Here I am using Philip Henderson's Everyman's Library edition in the *Shorter Novels of the Seventeenth Century*. London: Dent, 1967, pp. 147-224.

6. Important background is to be found in Frank Lestringan "Le Cannibale et ses Paradoxes," *Mentalities/Mentalite* 1:2, 1983.

7. Lestringan argues that the discovery and reporting of anthropologies by European voyagers in the Renaissance coincides with and develops out of the use of cannibalism as a polemical *topos* in the religious wars between Catholics and Protestants. The main insight we are drawing on rests in the view of the New World as a screen for projecting, condensing, revealing European fantasies otherwise beyond and below the range of verbal and image articulation. See also, Todorov, pp. 179-180.

8. One thinks immediately here of La Malinche (Doña Marina) and her role in Cortes's conquest of Mexico. (See Todorov, p. 100.)

9. Mrs. Behn is the first novelist cited by Lennard J. Davis in his discussion of how the term "novel" destabilizes and arises from the socially ambiguous stage of the real textualization of experience in the course of the seventeenth century; and only then does he go on to mention Daniel Defoe. (See Davis, p. 120.)

10. For second surveys of this problem see H. A. Hargreaves, "New Evidence of the Realism of Mrs. Behn's *Oroonoko*," *Bulletin of the New York Public Library* 74 (1970), 437-444; Martine Watson Brownley, "The Narrator in *Oroonoko*," *Essays in Literature* (Western Illinois University) 4 (1977), 174-181; and Angeline Goreau, *Reconstructing Aphra: A Social Biography of Aphra Behan Behn* (New York: Oxford University Press, 1980).

11. Goreau, pp. 62-63.

12. *Ibid.*, p. 290.

13. *Ibid.*, p. 58.

THE STRANGE CASE OF VLADIMIR NABOKOV AS A TRANSLATOR

Elizabeth Welt Trahan
(The Monterey Institute for International Studies)

Vladimir Nabokov was an avid chess player. His short novel *The Defense* (1964) is a chess player's story, and his collection *Poems and Problems* (1970) includes 18 chess problems, composed between 1940 and 1970. It also contains a telling remark by Nabokov that "[chess] problems are the poetry of chess."[1]

Nabokov's entire creative output seems to be one endless game of chess, and, paradoxically, also an enormous jigsaw puzzle. It is cerebral like chess, infinitely inventive, full of tricks and surprise moves and options, but also whimsically inconsistent and arbitrary, with a puzzle's interwoven random curves and arabesques: on both counts, a critic's joy and despair.

Translation contributes an important figure to Nabokov's literary chess game, one constantly on the move, manipulated by its master; it also provides a strange, elusive and at the same time pervasive pattern for his giant jigsaw puzzle. Critics have given some of their attention to various aspects of Nabokov's translation process and theory. However, the strange case of Vladimir Nabokov as a translator still needs to be assessed.[2]

Some basic facts will delineate the nature, scope and complexity of the "case."

Nabokov was born in Russia in 1899 and died in Switzerland in 1977. He grew up with Russian, English and French, according to his own recollections.[3] When the family fled Russia in 1919 and settled in Berlin, Vladimir went to Cambridge University for three years, studying Russian and French literature. Perhaps somewhat unsure of his English, if we may take our clue from *The Real Life of Sebastian Knight*, he was apparently not at any major linguistic disadvantage.[4] In Berlin between 1922 and 1937 Nabokov wrote, in Russian and under the pen name Vladimir Sirin, two volumes of poetry, two collections of short stories and nine novels. He likewise translated Lewis Carroll's *Alice in Wonderland* into Russian. This Sirin/Nabokov acquired a considerable reputation as a Russian émigré writer. At that time, Nabokov also began to write his autobiography. A story called "Mademoiselle O" was published in 1939 —interestingly in French.[5]

From 1937 to 1941 Nabokov lived in France. There he wrote (in Russian) the play *The Waltz Invention* (1938), and also began a novel in English, *The Real Life of Sebastian Knight*. In addition to writing poetry, he also translated extensively into Russian: poems by Supervielle, Tennyson, Yeats, and Verlaine (the translations are not extant); a novel by Romain Rolland as well as poems by Rupert Brooke, Ronsard, S. O'Sullivan (1922); *Alice in Wonderland*, Byron, Keats (1923); poems by Baudelaire (1927), Musset and Rimbaud (1928), two Shakespeare sonnets (1927) and a scene from *Hamlet* (1930), Goethe's Prolog to *Faust* (1932).[6] Finally, he translated several Pushkin poems into French (1937), an activity which, according to his biographer, Nabokov "now recalls with a moan."[7]

Meanwhile, one of Nabokov's Russian novels, *Camera Obscura* (1933), was published in English in London, in 1936.[8] Nabokov, dissatisfied with the translation, published his own in 1938—and another considerably reworked translation in 1960—changing the book's title to *Laughter in the Dark*. He likewise made his own translation of *Otchayanie* (1936), again in two versions. *Despair* was published in London in 1937, to be followed by a second, thoroughly revised translation (New York 1965, London 1966).[9] The remaining seven of Nabokov's nine Russian novels only became available in English after *Lolita* had brought him fame, money and notoriety. Though none of these translations were made by Nabokov himself, they were, nevertheless, very much his own: Nabokov charged his translators—his son Dmitri, and Michael Scammell and Michael Glenny, two Englishmen—with preparing totally literal renderings, reserving to himself the exclusive right to change anything.[10] Dmitri prepared *Invitation to a Beheading* (1959), *The Eye* (1965), *King, Queen, Knave* (1968), *Glory* (1972), the play *The Waltz Invention* (1966), some 25 stories and chapter one of *The Gift* (1963); Scammell prepared *The Gift* (chapters 2-5) and *The Defense* (1964); Glenny prepared *Mary* (1970). Dmitri's manuscripts are not available but the drafts prepared by Scammell and Glenny are, so that a comparison with the published versions could be—and was—made.[11] Some of its findings will be discussed in this paper.

In 1941 Nabokov moved to the United States. He taught at Wellesley until 1948 and at Cornell until 1958/9—the years of *Lolita*. Thereafter Nabokov resided in Switzerland. During his American period, he published four novels, *The Real Life of Sebastian Knight* (1941), *Bend Sinister* (1947), *Pnin* (1957), *Lolita* (Paris 1955, New York 1958, London 1959), and his autobiography, first serialized (*Atlantic Monthly*, January 1943, *The New Yorker*, January 1948-April 1950, *Partisan Review* and *Harper's*, 1951), then, in book form as *Speak Memory, a Memoir* (London 1951), and as *Conclusive Evidence: A Memoir* (New York 1951). His own Russian translation of the autobiography, *Drugie Berega*, appeared in 1954; finally, a new English edition, again considerably revised, appeared as *Speak Memory: An Autobiography Revisited* (London 1966, New York 1967).

In addition, the years in America also yielded a book of criticism, several short story collections, three major translations, and essays documenting the crystallization process of Nabokov's "translation theory."

The critical study *Gogol* (1944) was obviously meant as a corollary to Nabokov's teaching, which undoubtedly also provided the impetus for his translations of Lermontov's *A Hero of Our Time* (1958, with Dmitri), *The Song of Igor's Campaign* (1960) and Pushkin's *Eugene Onegin* (prepared 1950-54, published London and New York, 1964). An early transaltion of *Igor* which Nabokov used with his students at Cornell, he later dismissed as "a much too readable version" and urged that "copies of that obsolete version .... should now be destroyed."[12] In a similar vein, he considered his translation of three rhymed stanzas from chapter 1 of *Onegin*, which had appeared in the *Russian Review* in 1945, as an embarrassment whenever discussing his *Onegin* translation. He likewise disowned a slim volume of poetry translations from Pushkin, Lermontov and Tyutchev which he had published in 1944.[13] Yet, the earlier mentioned volume *Poems and Problems* contains in addition to the chess problems, to 39 Russian poems written between 1919 and 1967, and to 14 English poems dated 1942-1957, English versions of all the Russian poems included. Nor do these conform any more than the disowned translations mentioned above to the theory of literalness which, since approximately 1955, Nabokov proclaimed loudly and with increasing virulence and repetitiveness, in articles, prefaces and commentaries.[14]

Nabokov's theory of translation is based on his conviction that a) a good translation is an impossibility, b) a free translation is a travesty, and c) the only justification for a translation is its usefulness as a crib or pony, as he called it, for the serious student; therefore it must be as literal as possible and accompanied by as extensive a critical apparatus as the translator can muster. The translator must "produce with absolute exactitude the whole text and nothing but the text," and anything but a literal translation is "not truly a translation but an imitation, an adaptation or a parody."[15] In his Foreword to *Onegin*, Nabokov defines literal translation as "rendering, as closely as the associative and syntactical capacities of another language allow, the exact contextual meaning of the original,"[16] a statement reiterated in the Commentary and elsewhere.[17]

Nabokov is not the first nor the last to see translation as the reverse side of a tapestry, or to object to the translator's becoming a "re-creator" of a work of art. What is new is the extreme to which he takes this position: "In point of fact, any translation that does *not* sound like a translation is bound to be inexact upon inspection,"[18] or "I want translations with copious footnotes, footnotes reaching up like skyscrapers to the top of this or that passage so as to leave only the gleam of one textual line between the commentary and eternity,"[19] or "My Onegin falls short of the ideal crib. It is still not close enough and not ugly enough."[20] Finally, though Nabokov's four-volume translation of *Eugene Onegin* (Bollingen edition) consists of 256 pages of text and 1,175 pages of explication and commentary, Nabokov promises, upon preparing a new edition, that it "will be even more gloriously and monstrously literal than the first."[21]

The opening quatrain of *Eugene Onegin* can provide us with an excellent example of Nabokov's intentions and results. Here is first the original, transliterated and prosodically accented:

> Moy dyádya sámïh chéstnïh právil,
> Kogdá ne v shútku zanemóg,
> On uvazhát' sebyá zastávil,
> I lúchshe vídumat' ne móg . . . .

As "paraphrased" by Nabokov (i.e., a *bad* translation):

> My uncle, in the best tradition,
> By falling dangerously sick
> Won universal recognition
> And could devise no better trick . . . .

Nabokov's "lexical or constructional translation" (i.e., less bad):

> My uncle [is] of most honest rules [:]
> when not in jest [he] has been taken ill,
> he to respect him has forced [one],
> and better invent could not . . . .

And finally Nabokov's literal translation which he used in print:

> My uncle has most honest principles:
> when he was taken ill in earnest,
> he had made one respect him
> and nothing better could invent . . . .[22]

Nabokov's message is clear enough. Nor is it surprising that the publication of his *Onegin* translation elicited a storm of protest and polemic,[23] that the ensuing controversy with Edmund Wilson ended a friendship of long standing,[24] and that, to this day, Nabokov scholars and admirers—among then his son—continue to defend his *Onegin* translation and the rationale behind it. What they seem to have overlooked is the clue given by Nabokov's *tone* in the just quoted passages. It is the tone which we know from the many

Forewords and Afterwords and from the novels—Nabokov's teasing stance, ironic, exaggerating and defiant, full of baroque whimsy and cerebral arrogance—Nabokov's "Laughter from the Dark."[25]

The tone clues us in to the fact that Nabokov, despite his ascerbic attacks and counterattacks in the *Onegin* debate, was sublimely indifferent to notions of consistency and would, at his pleasure and to his own timing, devise and remake the rules of his chess game, of his "poetry of chess."

And indeed, if we now take a cursory glance at Nabokov's translations—our task is aided by much groundwork done by others[26]— we find that Nabokov felt quite free to shape and modify his translation technique as he saw fit, his theory notwithstanding.

Nabokov's translations seem to fall into several groups. His translation technique varies somewhat within and considerably between these groups.

The first group comprises the three prose translations, *A Hero of Our Time, The Song of Igor's Campaign,* and *Eugene Onegin.* They probably spawned Nabokov's theory and exemplify it best. Especially in *Onegin* literalness is surely carried to the extreme. Nabokov claims that in its totality his English *Onegin* conveys the totality of the Russian poem and at least one critic, Larry Gregg, seems to agree with him.[27] But Gregg also speaks of the translation as an "act of glorious pedantry,"[28] and of Nabokov as a "footnote-drugged maniac."[29] Since I personally like to think of Nabokov as primarily a stylist—and an outstanding one at that—I found *Onegin* deeply disappointing. I also believe that a combintation of extraneous factors may have pushed Nabokov toward literalness, until, eventually, their weight was transformed into a justification by him. There was first the need for a literal and heavily annotated version of *Eugene Onegin* to be used with his students; then Nabokov's propensity for pedantry and toward ferreting out odd bits of information; his penchant for discomfiting the critic and startling the reader; perhaps also his impatience with the enormous task which a verse translation presented; finally, his desire to present himself as a serious scholar to the many who saw in him only the author of *Lolita.*

The second group encompasses a number of translations supervised or made by Nabokov: the short stories and his one play available in English (both prepared by Dmitri), the majority of the Russian novels (*Despair* version I, translated by Vladimir Nabokov; *The Gift,* translated by Dmitri and Scammell; *The Defense,* translated by Scammell; *Invitation to a Beheading,* translated by Dmitri; *Glory,* translated by Dmitri; and *Mary,* translated by Glenny), as well as Nabokov's translation of *Lolita* into Russian (1967). In all of these translations, the changes made by Nabokov are slight and largely limited to stylistic improvements, minor structural changes, minor clarifications, specifications of time or date, a few minor additions and deletions.[30] Nabokov's theory of literalness echoes through these works in a minor key. So, for instance, Glenny translates a passage from *Mary*, somewhat freely, as follows: "The other chair . . . had disappeared under a black coat which lay there so clumsily and untidily that it might have been a piece of flotsom." Nabokov changes this to the clumsier but very literal "whose collapse seemed as heavy and shapeless as if it had fallen from the top of Mt. Ararat."[31]

Even funnier is the following passage, likewise from *Mary*. In a description of the protruding air vents on the roofs of railway carriages, Glenny abandons Nabokov's metaphor, "such'i soski," and settles conservatively for "ventilators." Nabokov promptly writes to him: "There are no 'revolving ventilators' in my text. 'Such'i soski' are 'dog's nipples'." And indeed, the final text reads: "Olive-drab carriages with a row of dark dog-nipples along their roofs."[32]

The third group comprises translations made by Nabokov or edited by him, which contain substantial changes. Here belong Nabokov's *Laughter in the Dark* and the second version of *Despair* (1965), Dmitri's *King, Queen, Knave* and *The Eye* and, finally (with the most extensive changes), Nabokov's various versions of his autobiography.

Within this group, Nabokov's handling of difficult passages is especially illuminating. As before, he might choose to be stubbornly literal. At other times, he would use ingenious equivalents of which any translator would be proud, as when translating "Chto delaet sovetskiy veter v slove veterinar?" as "What is this jest in majesty?"[33] And now and then, even Nabokov tends to drop a pun without an explanation, as when translating the multivalent title "Zashchita Luzhina" simply as "The Defense."[34]

It need not surprise us to find especially many differences between the authobiography's three versions. New material is added once Nabokov, back in Europe, is able to talk to old friends and family members and can extend his recall. But there are also interesting culturally predicated changes: the Russian version is far more critical of Germany and France than either of the English versions. Finally, while some of the extensive additions to the Russian translation are retained in the subsequent English version, others are again deleted.

As Grayson shows convincingly, no clear cut overall pattern emerges in Nabokov's translation practice. Some books are changed immediately, others years later. While some weak books were barely touched, some fascinatingly complex ones are repeatedly revised. In general, there seems to be a tendency toward greater precision of detail, tightening of thematic and symbolic devices, but also an increase in irony and aloofness, and an increase in artifice. It seems that Nabokov, always a compulsive reviser, uses the occasion of a translation as he would use that of a new edition, namely, to omit, add, change or refine. Once satisfied that the translation submitted to him meets the criterion of literalness, he now chooses to change, now to remain literal.

In Nabokov's later English novels, a rather unusual translation device makes its appearance. Already during his early years in Paris, Nabokov had often been accused of "foreignness," of being "un-Russian" in his choice of plots, and also of an overly elaborate language and extreme critical distance to his characters.[35] Later, perhaps because he is now sure of his footing and stature, Nabokov tends to assert this "foreignness" deliberately. His characters often speak Russian, English and French, switching from one language to another; transliterated Russian words and phrases are used with increasing frequency; and translation itself may give rise to puns, as when, in *Transparent Things*, Nabokov has one character say "yellow blue tibia," meaning the Russian "ya lyublyu tibya"—I love you.[36]

The final group consists of Nabokov's poetry, both that of his early translations from the Russian and the English versions he made of his own Russian poems. Despite many disclaimers, Nabokov seems to have translated his Russian verse by happily combining precision and closeness to the text with attention to rhythm, imagery and even rhyme whenever possible—and at times even at the expense of meaning, despite his insistence that meaning must precede form. Though his book *Poems and Problems* only contains two poems written after 1955 and his translations there are undated, I take the fact of the volume's publication in 1970 to indicate Nabokov's approval of its contents at that late date.[37]

It seems then that Nabokov is applying his theory of heavily annotated literalness only in two instances: 1. when he is translating other writers, primarily for the purpose of teaching their works ("The greatest reward I can think of is that students may use my work as a pony," he writes in his introduction to *Eugene Onegin*[38]) and 2. when demanding literal translations from his translators upon which he then imposes his own stylistic stamp and textual emendations with total freedom.

What price glory—in translation? we may ask at this point. Despite his admirers' insistence, Nabokov's *Eugene Onegin*, the most consistent demonstration of his theory of literal translation, is esthetically a failure, even if we see it, with Gregg, as "a glorious act of pedantry." Nabokov seems to have opted for glory of a monstrous kind, as perverse as that which he sought when writing *Lolita*, in defiance of the establishment and the reader: glory through a display of great verbal brilliance, and, in *Onegin*'s case, erudition, yet both of them negated by being made into tools toward erotic or scholarly exhibitionism.

Fortunately, Nabokov's deeds belie his words—at least now and then. Whether from arrogance or modesty, he had chosen to forego the glory of translation as a re-creation for the pedantry of antiquarian erudition. But his innate propensity for translating—and Nabokov is, beyond a doubt, a born translator—kept asserting itself. Thus, whenever Nabokov ignored his own theory and his own cynicism about the possibility of translation—or did he merely allow his good business sense to prevail?—his remarkable linguistic and stylistic talents produced English translations which are, in their verbal felicity, peers to the works Nabokov wrote in Russian.

NOTES

1. Vladimir Nabokov, *Poems and Problems* (New York, London: McGraw Hill, 1970), p. 15.

2. Cf. Bevery Lyon Clark, "Nabokov's Assault on Wonderland," *Nabokov's Fifth Arc*, ed. Rivers & Nicol (Austin, Texas: 1982), pp. 63-74; Robert P. Hughes, "Notes on the Translation of *Invitation to a Beheading*," *Nabokov*. ed. Appel & Newman (London: 1971), pp. 284-292; D. Barton Johnson, "Contrastive Phonoaesthetics or Why Nabokov Gave Up Translating Poetry as Poetry," *A Book of Things about Vladimir Nabokov*, ed. C. R. Proffer (Ann Arbor: 1974), pp. 28-41; C. R. Proffer, "From *Otchaianie* to *Despair*," *Slavic Review*, June 1965; C. R. Proffer, *Keys to Lolita* (Bloomington, Indiana: 1968); Earl D. Sampson's introductory remarks to V. Nebokov's "Postscript to the Russian Edition of *Lolita*," *Nabokov's Fifth Act*, pp. 188-190. Finally, the most important work on the subject, Jane Grayson's *Nabokov Translated. A Comparison of Nabokov's Russian and English Prose* (Oxford University Press, 1977).

3. Cf. V. Nabokov's Foreword to *Drugie Beraga* (New York, 1954), p. 7; and his Foreword to *Strong Opinions* (McGraw Hill, 1974), p. 5.

4. Cf. V. Nabokov, *The Real Life of Sebastian Knight* (London:

1964), pp. 27, 40-41.

5. It appeared in *Mesures* (Paris: 1939). An English translation, by Hilda Ward, with Nabokov's revisions, was published in the January 1943 issue of the *Atlantic Monthly*. It became, with further revisions by Nabokov, chapter five of the Autobiography. The story is also included in *Nine Stories* (1947) and in *Nabokov's Dozen* (1958).

6. Cf. Grayson, pp. 244-245.

7. Cf. Andrew Field, *Nabokov. His Life in Art* (New York: 1967), p. 266.

8. The translator was Winifred Roy. The novel originally appeared in serial form in *Sovremennye zapiski* (Paris: 1932-33).

9. Written in Berlin in 1932, it, too, was first serialized in *Sovremennye zapiski* (1934) and appeared in book form in Berlin in 1936. The second English version was serialized in *Playboy* in 1965-66;

10. Cf. Grayson, p. 8.

11. Grayson, *passim*.

12. Grayson, p. 18.

13. V. Nabokov, *Three Russian Poets* (Norfolk, Conn.).

14. Cf. "Problems of Translation: *Onegin* in English," *Partisan Review*, XXII, Fall 1955, 496-512; "Zametki perevodchika" (A Translator's Notes), *Novy Zhurnal*, XLIX, 1957, 130-144; "Zametki perevodchika II," *Opyty* VIII, 1957, 36-49; "The Servile Path," *On Translation*, ed. R. Brower (Cambridge, Mass. 1959). Cf. also, among others, Nabokov's Forewords to *A Hero of Our Time* and to *Eugene Onegin*, and his Commentary to *Onegin*.

15. "Problems of Translation: *Onegin* in English," p. 496.

16. Alexander Pushkin, *Eugene Onegin*, tr. Vladimir Nabokov (New York and London: 1964), I, p. viii.

17. *Ibid.*, III, p.185; "Reply to my Critics," *Encounter* (London)

February 1966 (reprinted in *Vladimir Nabokov: Nabokov's Congeries*, ed. Page Stegner, New York: 1968, pp. 300-324; and in *Strong Opinions*, pp. 241-267).

18. Iuri Lermontov, *A Hero of Our Time*, tr. Vladimir Nabokov in collaboration with Dmitri Nabokov (New York: 1958), p. xii.

19. "Problems of Translation: *Onegin* in English," p. 512.

20. V. Nabokov, "Reply to my Critics," quoted from *Strong Opinions*, pp. 242-243.

21. Grayson, pp. 15-16.

22. All three translations and Nabokov's terminology as stated are quoted from his *Onegin*, I, pp. vii-ix.

23. Cf. V. Nabokov, "On Translating Pushkin: Pounding the Clavichord," *New York Review of Books*, April 30, 1964, pp. 14-16; Walter Arndt, "A Reply to Vladimir Nabokov: Goading the Pony," *ibid.*, p. 16; V. Nabokov, "Postscript to W. Arndt's article 'Goading the Pony'," *ibid.*

24. Cf. Edmund Wilson, "The Strange Case of Pushkin and Nabokov," *New York Review of Books*, July 15, 1965, pp. 3-6, and V. Nabokov, "Reply to my Critics."

25. Cf. Elizabeth W. Trahan, "Laughter from the Dark: A Memory of Vladimir Nabokov," *Antioch Review*, Spring 1985.

26. Cf. Note 2.

27. Cf. L. Gregg, "Slava Snabokovu," *A Book of Things about Vladimir Nabokov*, pp. 10-25 (originally published in *Russian Literature Triquarterly*, v. 3, 313-329).

28. *A Book of Things*, p. 18.

29. *Ibid.*, p. 19.

30. Grayson gives an excellent, detailed discussion of Nabokov's translations and their relationship to the originals.

31. V. Nabokov, *Mary* (New York: 1970), p. 23. The original reads:

"Drugoi stul . . . ischezal pod chornym pidzhakom, pavshim na nego slovno s Ararata, tak on tyazhelo i ryzhno sel." (Vladimir Sirin, *Mashenka*, Berlin: 1926; reprinted as Vladimir Nabokov, *Mashenka*, by Ardis/McGraw Hill in 1974), p. 39.

32. *Mary*, p. 10.

33. *Otchayanie* (Paris and Berlin: 1936), p. 111, and *Despair* (New York: 1965), p. 131.

34. The Russian title suggests 1. a specific chess move, 2. "Luzhin's defense" and 3. "In defense of Luzhin."

35. Cf. Grayson, pp. 234-237 and Ludmilla A. Foster, "Nabokov in Russian Emigre Criticism," *Russian Literature Triquarterly* v. 3, 330. 341.

36. V. Nabokov, *Transparent Things* (London: 1975), p. 52.

37. Nabokov's introduction to the book speaks of "only one little compromise I have accepted: whenever possible, I have welcomed rhyme, or its shadow." (*Poems and Problems*, p. 14). So be it. Providing evidence to the contrary would comprise another essay.

38. *Onegin*, I, p. x.

Review of National Literatures
ABSTRACTS

A R M E N I A (Volume 13)
Special Editor: Vahe Oshagan

ANNE PAOLUCCI, "Armenia's Literary Heritage: National Focus and Universal Receptiveness," pp. 15-27.

The Armenian language has the rare distinction of having acquired a written form, with its own distinct alphabet, not so much for the purposes of "written self-expression," as to permit its students, young and old, to study and cherish as their own the contents of the best writings in other ancient languages. The Armenians had been a literate people, reading and writing Greek, which they loved, and Syriac, which has been the language of conquerors. The chief concern was to have the Holy Scriptures of Christianity in a written language of their own; but with those Scriptures came also master works of Church fathers and other books of Christian interest in Greek and Syriac. The art of translation, for which the written language was invented c. 400 AD, reached great heights of perfection almost instantly, turning newly-written Armenian at once into a translator's language par excellence. That accounts for the flowering of a classical, written Armenian literature with almost unbelievable rapidity—there being little evidence of *any* non-sophisticated writing in Armenian at any time before the long centuries of subjection to foreign powers. Interestingly, after centuries of decline, it was once again a desire to translate foreign masterpieces that brought on a modern parallel to the first classical flowering of original Armenian written literature. This time, the catalyst was Shakespeare. Again, there were "holy translators" (starting with Hovhannes Mahseyan—or Massehian—who died in 1931) and continuing to the present. Like the ancient Armenian translators of Christian Scriptures, the learned Rouben Zarian has aptly said, the modern Armenian translators of Shakespeare have permitted the "language of a small trodden nation" to earn for itself "the right to stand on an equal footing with that of a developed nation."

VAHE OSHAGAN, "A Brief History of Armenian Literature," pp. 28-44.

The modern epoch of Armenian literature dates from the closing decades of the 18th century when political events, in effect, split the Armenian nation into two:—the Eastern Armenians, who included those living in the Russian empire, India, Persia, and the Far East; and the Western Armenians, living en masse in the Ottoman Empire and the rest of the world. Notably, each of these divisions developed under a different foreign influence: the Eastern Armenians under Russia and the Western Armenians under a European, predominantly French influence. Tiflis, in time, became the cultural capital of the Eastern Armenians, and Constantinople of the Western Armenians. Just as the first flowering of a written Armenian literature, centuries before, had had a powerful religious or ecclesiastical base, so, again, there were powerful Church initiatives in printing, translating, and teaching carried on for decades by the enlightened Patriarchs, in Constantinople, Venice, and Vienna. In this second renaissance, however, the Armenian interest in Shakespeare proved a powerful stimulus, doing for modern Armenian literature what the parallel interest of the Germans in Shakespeare in the age of Herder and Goethe did for modern German literature. Much of the history of modern Armenian literature has been the effort to bridge the gap between the divergent tendencies of Eastern and Western Armenian literature. There have been parallel movements, crowding century-long changes into decades and years. And there have been political disasters that have brought on immense, traumatic, cultural-spiritual shocks. There are hopeful years, however, in East and West, fresh literary identities are emerging—especially in the United States portion of the Western diaspora.

ELENA ALEXANIAN, "19th Century Armenian Realism and its International Relations," pp. 45-63.

Critical thinking and the realist attitude in East Armenian literature began about 1860, some 25 years after the triumph of the Russian naturalist school headed by N. Gogol. The first writer to be affected by this change in Russian letters was Alexander Soundoukian, and the effect was especially noticeable in his treatment of "domestic plays" and prose works. Soundoukian focused on the portrayal of moral vices and social ills. Striking was his treatment of the *middle woman*, so important in the theater of Gogol and Ostrovski. Soundoukian's art consists of "armenizing" such stock characters, all the while remaning very European in his skillful handling of dialogue, his critique of society and his satirical verve. The true master of satire, however, remains Hagop Baronian, whose *Baghdassar Aghpar* (Brother Baghdassar) combines a hilarious situation with a sober moral message, an encounter that gives rise to a phantasm. This was the time Armenian critical realism blossomed, unveiling the social ills of the age and projecting into the literary scene a new character—"the little man" or the underdog. It was in the final redemption of this character that the Armenians saw the triumph of humanism. With Havannes Tumanian there is a further identification of the "little man" with the common people; his short story "Kikor" embodies the pathos of Armenian suffering, giving it universal resonance. With Alexandre Shirvanzade, middle class values, human alienation, exploitation, loss of identity, social contradictions found their way into the major literary forms of the time. In his novelette *The Artist* he drew upon Maupassant and Chekhov—the two main sources of his inspiration. Chekhov figures as a major influence in Nar-Toss, also—an important prose writer and a bitter critic of the "immoral," dehumanizing bourgeoisie. The novels of Nar-Toss, such as *Anna Saroyan*, not only analyze the results of the loss of identity and moral values but also describe in great detail the psychological dynamics of the prerevolutionary era. The West Armenian writer Krikor Zohrab too had a close artistic affinity with Maupassant and Chekhov. The moral problematics and psychological dramatic structure of Ibsen and Chekhov also left their mark on Armenian dramatists like Shirvanzade and Soundoukian—especially in the depicting of themes of loneliness and spiritual solitude. The work of these two Armenian writers helped to define the artistic innovations of the "new theatre." The plays of Levon Shant deal with the clash of real and ideal, the profane and the sacred. He too grappled with the drama of solitary men who are highly critical of society and yet filled with passion for life itself. What Shant's theater brings into focus through his psychological dramas is ultimately the Armenian national reality within the larger context of universal problems.

JAMES ETMEKJIAN, "Western European and Modern Armenian Literary Relations up to 1915," pp. 64-92.

Western Armenian literature has been influenced by the four major Western literatures: English, German, Italian, and French. Early contacts with English culture started in India in the 17th and

18th centuries, continued in Venice during Byron's stay with the Mekhitarists (1816-17) and the translation of *Robinson Crusoe* in 1817, followed by the translation of *Paradise Lost* in 1824. More telling than Byron's influence on the Mekhitarists, however, was the strong British presence in Constantinople and the arrival of the protestant missionaries in the early 19th century, both producing a lasting effect on the Armenians through the anglophile masses created by the hundreds of schools, colleges, churches opened by American missionaries. In terms of purely literary influence, English romanticism pervaded Armenian letters later in the century, especially Byron's writings, the poetry of R. Vorperian and the translations of Swift, Goldsmith, and Sir Walter Scott. But the most powerful influence was that exerted by Shakespeare's plays, which the Smyrna-based Dedeyan Press began to publish in 1853. This continuing interest in Shakespeare gave a certain permanence to English influence and presence among the Armenians. German influence was less widespread; it infiltrated into West Armenian letters through the Romantic writers like Goethe, Schiller and later Heine—all of whom were very popular especially among those who had studied with the German missions in the Provinces. Italian influence centered mainly around the Mekhitarist congregation (established in Venice in 1717), through their schools, publications, and translations—among which Metastasio's moralistic plays found great favor, as did Alfieri's plays (*Saul, Merope* [trans. 1873]). Foscolo and Monti were also translated, but the "krapar" classical Armenian used in the translations limited their impact. French influences were the greatest, both on Armenian writers and the general public, starting in the 1840s (with Armenian students who went to Paris and were impressed with Hugo, Lamartine, Musset, etc. and carried their enthusiasm back into Armenian life, translating literally hundreds of works by classical and romantic French authors (Molière, Pascal, Voltaire, Rousseau, Lamartine, Chateaubriand and scores of others). The most popular figure was Victor Hugo, the object of a veritable cult. (At his death, many Armenian schools were closed.) French Romantic literature was clearly a major influence in the aesthetic formation of many West Armenian poets, such as Tourian, Beshigtashlian, Terzian, Stian, and novelists like Hissarian and Dussap. With the advent of Realism, French influence continued through Daudet, Maupassant, Zola, and Coppée. Prose writers like Zohrab, Yeroukhan, Yessayan (and poets like Siamanto, Tekeyan, Varouzhan, Medrents) strongly responded to the French impact.

VARAK NERSISSIAN, "Medieval Armenian Poetry and its Relation to Other Literatures," pp. 93-120.

The roots of medieval Armenian poetry reach down deep into the pre-Christian culture and the celebrated Koghtn Songs. With the adoption of Christianity in the fourth century, however, these pagan songs were replaced by religious songs called *sharagans* that dominated the musical scene for six centuries. Yet such was the strength of the popular spirit that permeated them that these pagan songs resurfaced in most unexpected ways, such as in the strong non-religious elements in the poetry of the tenth-century mystic poet Krikor Naregatsi. "A poetry of nature and of love" says M. Apeghian "that laid the foundation of the new lyricism of medieval times." It is essentially secular poetry expressed in the popular vernacular that, aided by major social changes and economic upheavaals, finally triumphed and emerged into the open, between the thirteenth and sixteenth centuries, through the works of such poets as Frig, Hovannes Blouz, Constantine Yerzengatsi, Mgrditch Naghash and others. These men are sons of the people and the true product of their times. One of them, the famous Frig, even draws close to a political stand in his poem "Complaint," inspired by the suffering of his people. Another theme that received special attention was that of the migrant laborer or "gharib" yearning for affection and suffering all alone, as portrayed in the poetry of Mgrditch Naghash. But it was the theme of love which, in typical oriental fashion, exercised the greatest attraction on poets like Constantine Yerzengatsi, Hovannes Toulgourantsi, Krikor Aghtamartsi, and others. The greatest of them was Nahabed Kouchag, whose love poetry is "the crown of medieval Armenian verse"; his innovation consists in treating the woman not merely as an object of desire but also and especially as a human being with her own will and personality. All these poets entertained extensive contacts with neighboring cultures, in particular with Turkish and Persian poetry from which Hovannes Blouz did some translations too. The same is true for Frig. Certain themes and genres such as the allegory of the Rose and the Nightingale or the ancient epic Shahname, known to fifth-century Armenian historian Movses Khorenatsi, exercised a special influence on poets like Constantine Yerzengatsi, Arakel Paghishetsi, Mgrditch Naghash, Krikoris Aghtamartsi, Khatchadour Getcharetsi, Hovannes Toulgourantsi and others. The social poetry of Frig shows thematic affinities with the work of the 10th-century Persian poet Routaki, with Omar Khayyam's poetry and the writings of the 15th-century Turkish poetess Mehri Khatoun. The list is long and indicates the presence of a continuous and often fruitful interinfluence between Armenian medieval poets and the oriental poetic tradition of the peoples of the region.

BOGHOS LEVON ZEKIYAN, "Personal Tragedy and Cultural Backgrounds in the Poetry of Bedros Turian," pp. 121-149.

Armenian Romanticism appears first in the middle of the 19th century—more as an expression of national feeling than a reaction to classicism. The movement was spearheaded by Ghevond Alishan, Khatchadour Apovian, Megrditch Beshigtashlian and Bedros Turian —the last-named by far the most prominent poet of the group. Turian was poor, a precocious pupil, an avid reader of classical Armenian poetry, of translations of Rousseau, Bernadin de Saint-Pierre, Chateaubriand, Lamartine and Musset. He also believed staunchly in women's emancipation and held, for his time, avantgarde social and literary notions while remaining essentially a "romantic" poet. Turian's great achievement remains the forging of the poetic language of modern Western Armenia out of the popular vernacular of his day. In this, he owes much to his predecessors, especially to Armen Loussignan, some of whose figures of speech can be traced in Turian's poetry. But the similarity between the two poets ends there. Loussignan's writing served to prepare the way for the linguistic and stylistic innovations brought about by Turian. More evident is his dependence on Lamartine and Musset, although Turian is more spontaneous than the French poets. Turkish influences seem minimal; still, Turian shows extraordinary sensitivity in describing certain special situations, as in the poem "Trkouhin," which contains some of his best love imagery. More pronounced appears to be Turian's affinity with the imagery and direct dramatic expression of love found in the work of the 18th-century troubador Sayat Nova. Turian's vision of the ideal Armenian woman—especially in his representation of Armenian ladies in the *History of Vartan*— seems to have been influenced by the 5th-century historian-writer Yeghishe. Another source of inspiration was the 10th-century poet Gregory of Nareg, whose religious imagery and poetic patterns are often found in Turian's work. His life was one long tragedy: poverty, social discrimination, and disdain by the wealthy, loneliness, extreme timidity, physical frailty and general ill-health and finally tuberculosis and, not least, his anguished concern for his country, which he saw deprived of freedom and suffering in subjection, brought about his early death. Thus, for all its tenderness, Turian's poetry springs from a dark core of tragedy to which he gave admirable expression in his masterpiece, "Trtunchk," a perfect example of Max Jacob's comment "It is proper for lyricism to be unconscious, but an unconscious which is subject to control." Deep down, Turian remained a humanist. In his own words: "I am not a poet, but I love poetry . . . . I, who love poetry best in the world, would like that my last breath be also a poem . . . ." In this large poetic vision, there is a dimension of "silence" which points to the inner power of Turian's poetry.

HRAND TAMRAZIAN, "Yeghishe Charentz and the Socialist Revolution," pp. 150-173.

Yeghishe Charentz started his career as a melancholic, spell-bound poet and ended it as the powerful voice of the Socialist Revolution. The principal agent of this change was the Great War and the immense suffering of the Armenian people, both of which he experienced in full and which shattered his adolescent dream-world, giving rise, at the same time, to a new consciousness of himself and of what was, for him, the inevitable unity between the destiny of his country and that of the new world order. His early works betray his deeply lyrical nature, his unquenchable thirst for an ideal world which he calls Nairi or the Nairian world of his earliest ancestors, a mythical reality that will haunt him all his life. He is also a poet of the stark reality of Nature and human suffering, and it is the brutal shock of these two that spurs him on to his next stand, that of the poetry of protest. Thus, his vision of reality gradually becomes more tragic and, as he grows, he paints with more powerful, more violent colors the destruction of Armenia and the collapse of the old world. It is at this time that Charentz joins the ranks of the Revolutionary armies and turns into a Soldier-Poet, identified in body and spirit with the ideals of the Revolution. This is a crucial period in his life because as a revolutionary poet he feels compelled to initiate a totally new poetic style and to start a new tradition in Armenian poetry. His writings of this period seem to revive the dying national poetry through the powerful inspiration that he gets from the Revolution. This is the start of his Romantic period, the emergence of the heroic style and the appearance of that epic breadth with which he celebrates the March of the Frenzied Masses and the coming of the new Era of History. But for all his internationalism, Charentz could not dissociate his life and his talent from the tragic fate of his native country ravaged by the Turks. He returned to the capital, Yerevan, to help in its resurrection. The spectacle of chaos and suffering filled him with despair and inspired the celebrated *Mahvan Desil* (Vision of Death). With the coming of the Red Army into Armenia, this morbid vision gave way to a new hope for the future of his tormented, tiny land. In his short life, Charentz succeeded in opening up a new poetic world and create a poetry of work, struggle, and hope infused with broad philosophical implications.

LEVON HAKHVERDIAN, "Armenian National Drama and its International Context," pp. 174-193.

Armenian classical drama developed in the two major centers of Tiflis and Constantinople early in the 19th century. Of the scores of plays written at the time, three attract the attention of the modern critic and public: Kapriel Sountougian's *Bebo* (1871), Hagop Baronian's *Baghdassar Aghpar* (1886) and Alexandre Shirvanzade's *Badvi Hamar* (1905). The universal theme of *Bebo*—the comic drama of a simple, ordinary, active man pitted against a corrupt world which he can neither accept nor change—its solid realism and the pure working-class dialect in which it is written has made this the still unsurpassed masterpiece of Armenian dramatic literature. Baronian's *Baghdassar Aghpar* satirizes social norms within the setting of a traditional sentimental triangle, effectively portraying the pathos of an innocent husband constantly frustrated in his desperate efforts to state his side of the story, to tell the truth and to seek legal redress. Shirvanzade's *Badvi Hamar* is built around the theme of Man and Money and depicts with great psychological insight and dramatic skill of characterization the moral depravity of human beings carried away by a passion for material wealth. It is also a bitter attack against superstition and the obsolete moral rules that often cause much suffering in societies in transition. These plays are the product of the same critical attitude toward modern civilization that other writers like Avedick Issahakian in his *Abul Ala El Maari* (the dramatic poem inspired by the Arabic thinker), Levon Shant in his play *Hin Asdvadzner* (Ancient Gods), which depicts the violent conflict of mentalities, and Terenig Demirdjian in his *Katch Nazar* (Nazar the Brave), inspired by popular legend, have all echoed in their own way.

VAHE OSHAGAN, "Cosmopolitanism in West Armenian Literature," pp. 194-213.

Cosmopolitanism has always existed among the Armenians and in West Armenian literary life, in some form or other, perhaps as a result of their world-wide dispersion from the 14th century on. But they too, on their part, kept their minds and way of life open to all the currents in the world of ideas, particularly to the civilization of the Christian West. In this way, around the middle of the 19th century, the West Armenian elites and literati, concentrated mainly in Constantinople—the capital of the Ottoman Empire—fell under the influence of preromanticism, a literary movement with a European contour and a definitely cosmopolitan inspiration. This coincidence reinforced and brought out the cosmopolitan tendencies already latent in the Armenian way of thinking. Books like Fénelon's *Les Aventures de Télémaque, Paul et Virginie* by Bernardin de Saint-Pierre, *Night Thoughts* by Edward Young, Goethe's *Werther*, Silvio Pellico's *My Prisons* were translated into Armenian and gained great popularity, thus helping to propagate the spirit of multi-national literature which, in the absence of a strong ethnic literary tradition, became synonymous with "Westernization" and "modernization." But for all their enthusiasm for foreign cultures and their readiness to adopt a sympathetic attitude toward all Western literary values, the Armenians were on the whole unable to appreciate the basic philosophical notions of the cosmopolitan spirit to the full—such things as the concept of natural religion and natural morality, world literature, le mal-du-siecle of the romantic sensibility, etc. At a second level, we can see that the Armenian westernized men of letters were torn between two opposing forces pulling in different directions—on the one hand their close ties with the ethnic culture and their obligation to serve their nation, on the other the lure of foreign cultures leading to assimilation. Many did face this difficult choice and what they achieved can perhaps be called the "Armenian brand of cosmopolitanism." In other words, a sincere, intense, almost servile respect and love for all things spiritual coming from the West and an effort of emulation of literary models, best-sellers in vogue in the West. But although none of the Armenian writers has attained international stature, this cosmopolitanism, from the Armenian point of view, can be construed as an overflow of talent that attests to the literary energy of the nation. With hindsight, we can today note that some of the major cosmopolitan figures in Armenian letters such as Mateos Mamourian, Yeghia Demirdjibashian, Krikor Odian, Sirpouhi Dussap are way ahead of their contemporaries—to a great extent because of their cosmopolitan aspiration. Predictably, cosmopolitanism gave rise to reactions. A "return to ethnic values" took place around 1910, in itself a salutary event that might have flowered into something exceptional had not the Genocide of 1915 overtaken the Armenian nation. Another reaction was the total severance of ties with the ethnic background in favor of full commitment to a foreign literature. Such was the case with Charles Akdjalian, Bedros Tenger, Victoria Aghanoor-Pompili, Tigran Yergat, Hrand Nazariantz, Iskouhi Minas, and to a lesser degree, Sdepan Voskan, Kalousd Gosdantian, Gosdan Zarian and scores of others.

VREJ NERSESSIAN, "Bibliographical Spectrum on Modern Armenian Literature," pp. 214-237.

Early forms of Armenian literary histories began to be written around the middle of the 19th century in four important centers at once: the two Mekhitarist Monasteries, one in Venice and the other in Vienna; a third center in Kazan and a fourth in Tiflis. By the end of the century the genre had received considerable attention and had developed through the writings of such subjective historians as Leo and Manvelian in Eastern Armenia and Arpiarian in Western Armenia. The subjective and purely literary approach to the genre remained very popular with the Armenians all through the 10th century, culminating in the huge 12-volume *Panorama of West Armenian Literature* of Hagop Oshagan written between 1935 and 1948 and published between 1945 and 1984. Mian Toloyan's 2-volume *A Century of Armenian Literature* published recently is done in the same spirit but lacks Oshagan's depth and breadth of vision. Some scholars have adopted a more objective attitude and have transcended the Eastern-Armenian and Western-Armenian duality by working from a unifed point of reference. Such is the case of the histories of H. Adjarian, M. Apeghian and V. Papazian. The most ambitious and comprehensive, as well as the most successful achievement in this line remains however the 5-volume *History of Modern Armenian Literature* published between 1962 and 1979 by the Manoug Apeghian Institute of Literature in Yerevan. Literary criticism grew among the Armenians from around 1850 in conection with the vital issue of the creation of a literary language. Critics in both sections of the Armenian world, Kh. Apovian and S. Nazariants in the East and S. Voskanian and K. Odian and others in the West, waged bitter struggles for and against the use of Krapar. Finally, the popular vernaculars won, in both regions. Over the last 150 years, journals too have carried many of the debates about genres, foreign influences, themes, questions of national style, etc. In Soviet Armenia the issue of Socialist Realism and aesthetics has kept a great number of Marxist critics busy from the 1920s on. Critics like E. Chrbashian, S. Sarinian, A. Derderian, A. Garinian, H. Tamrazian and others have distinguished themselves in this field while writers like A. Chobanian, V. Oshagan and others have kept the interest in literary theory alive in the West. Anthologies in French or English are few in Armenian literature. The most important and best known in the English-speaking world are those of Alice Stone Blackwell's *Armenian Poems, Rendered into English Verse* (1917), *Anthology of Armenian Poetry* translated and edited by Diana Der Hovanessian and Marzabed Margossian (1978), Aram Tolegian's *Armenian Poetry Old and New* (1979), and *An Anthology of Western Armenian Literature* by James Etmekjian (1979). Among the Eastern Armenians, there are three anthologies in Russian published before the Revolution. A recent work by A. Ter-Hakopian, *Western Armenian Poetry* (1979), makes available to the Russian public the works of major West Armenian poets. The most important bibliographies are those published in Soviet Armenia, especially those of the Academy of Sciences in Yerevan, but the tradition goes back to 1883, to the Mekhitarists in Venice. A. Salmaslian's *Bibliographie de L'Armenie* (1969) is the only comprehensive book on Armenian literature and Armenians in foreign languages.

NISHAN PARLAKIAN AND HENRY PAOLUCCI, "Armenian Literature Between East and West," pp. 238-264.

More is still written in French and Russian about Armenian literature, both critically and appreciatively, than in English or the other European languages; but things are changing. In recent years translations into English have begun to flourish. In the critical instances there are a number of very good brief works in English by Diana Der Hovanessian and Marzabed Margossian, by R. W. Thomson, and, of another order, by Ara Baliozian. But we have yet to match the longer works in Italian, French, and German. Worthy of extensive examination in English are H. Thorossian's *Histoire de la littérature arménienne des origine jusqu'à nos jours* (Paris, 1951) and Vahan Inglisian's book-length "Die armenische Literatur," in *Handbuch der Orientalistik* (B. Spuler, ed., Part I, *Der nahe und der mittlere Osten,* Vol. VII, *Armenisch und kaukasische Sprachen* [Leiden/Koln, E. J. Brill, 1963]). Inglisian's history was completed just a year or two after Thorossian's (there was a delay in publication); and yet it seems to represent an altogether new age of critical scholarship and approach, as thoroughly Austrian/German as Thorossian's is traditionally French. Thorossian's account is always leisurely. Inglisian, on the contrary, gives us page after page crammed with information that deserves and rewards the most careful reading and study. The historical survey provided by Inglisian omits nothing, giving us in all its chapters a sense of having been brought up to date from the standpoint of scholarly research, with the fullest possible recognition and respect accorded the labors of Inglisian's predecessors. Thorossian structures the recent part of his history to permit himself to end with an account of Western Armenian literature, where he can stress parallels with the modernist tendency of Western European and American literature. Inglisian ends with an account of Soviet Armenian literature, which permits him to conclude that in the East, despite the restrictive ideology, "there at least exists a national state, and a consequent upsurge in every branch of spiritual life." In the Eastern Armenian sphere he concludes, "one even comes across Western Armenians, particularly from Van-Vaspurakan, of whom thousands came here for safety during World War I, and appropriated as their own the like manner of thinking and speaking of the Eastern Armenians. In today's Soviet Armenia, too, there are masters of the art of poetry who, not less than in earlier times, sing of their native land and its beauties." Inglisian there reminds his readers that the *national* impulse of an Armenian national literature is not lightly repressed, neither by a spurious ideology nor a hardly less spurious cosmopolitanism.

CNL: A "RETROSPECTIVE" (1974–1984)

Anne Paolucci
(President, CNL)

When *Review of National Literatures* was established in 1970, as a semi-annual, the only other major journal in the USA with a plural in its title was *Research in African Literatures*. At the time, a number of colleagues wrote to question the use of the plural in our title, but I was confident that it was a sound decision and that literary studies would eventually move into a larger area, beyond the established European spectrum, the traditional canon of English, French, Spanish, Italian, and German.

In time, over the years, my conviction has been proved sound. The established "comparative" canon, stemming from the common base of Greco-Roman culture, must always be the major source of our analytical methodologies and will surely continue to provide the basic structures for bringing together a number of literatures. I am aware, of course, of the kind of objection which has been raised, many times and always in the same way, about our inability or perhaps unwillingness to look at other literatures through any other kind of critical scrim. My answer, very simply—and it is in no way meant to be flippant or derogatory—is that "our" critical perspective is all we have: just as other experts from other literatures have *their* way of looking at literature. We may come to some adjustment in time (we *must* if there is to be productive exchange); but a Western-trained literary scholar can never dismantle his/her Greco-Roman heritage, the Aristotelian methodology (even when we disagree—to paraphrase another author—we do so at our own peril) which has shaped our thinking and provided us with the most fruitful approach to critical analysis and all its ramifications. What I would add in this argument is this: The European "comparative" spectrum can offer all of us an effective and proven "cluster" of the kind that we must try to map out for literatures not in the Western tradition or in the "European mainstream." Needless to say, our Greco-Roman cluster does have a common base (which is often taken for granted these days, especially by enthusiastic scholars who wish to move into "non-Western" literaty studies and end up picking up arbitrary experience without a flexible and expandable plan). India may have a similar common base; Africa, perhaps; the South Pacific countries—Australia and New Zealand especially—certainly may be considered in one grouping;—but in all such "other" clusters, there is *no common base of the kind found in the Greco-*

Roman inheritance of our European comparative literary tradition. This is a most important point to keep in mind; it accounts for the relative ease with which some Western scholars have moved into literary experiences outside the European mainstream and the difficulty experienced by other scholars schooled in narrower traditions, who have, as a consequence, not recognized the need for cultural "clustering" and comparative buttressing as basic to any experiment in multinational and global literary studies.

In 1974, the year before *RNL* began independent publication, CNL was launched as a non-profit educational foundation for *RNL* and other CNL publications, annual meetings, joint ventures with other institutions, panels, special projects and programs. My fondest memory of this difficult period of transition is the receipt in the mail one day of our very first paid membership from Harvard University.

Over the years, CNL has articulated its commitment to expand comparative literary studies in a variety of ways. Twice it was invited by Columbia University's School of International Affairs to provide a literary segment for their annual conference in Social Studies. (The presentations subsequently appeared as special publications by CNL: *Problems in National Literary Identity and the Writer as Social Critic* and *New Literary Continents*.) In 1981 CNL was invited to take part in the preparation of a 5-month NEH/Shakespeare Association of America "Shakespeare Summerfest" in New York City. That unforgettable program of exhibits, special features, lectures, professional theater, etc. included, also, every Saturday for the duration of the project (housed in The American Museum of Natural History) a number of CNL bilingual "mini-dramatizations/readings" from Shakespeare—each program with its own director and actors/readers. This extraordinary "mini series" called attention to the various reception of Shakespeare in such countries as Greece, Russia, Germany, Italy, Spain, Turkey, Japan, and France, and such cultures as Yiddish, Afro-American, and Armenian. Unfortunately, the series could not be preserved on videotape at the time; but summaries of two of the programs—Rosette Lamont's presentation of "The *Hamlet* Myth in French Literature" and Nishan Parlakian's masterful Armenian presentation featuring a brief survey of the Armenian response to Shakespeare, especially the excellent translations made into Armenian, and offering dramatic readings from *Othello, Lear,* and *Macbeth*—were published in the special *CNL/QWR* of October 1982.

In 1984, CNL celebrated its 10th anniversary in Washington D.C. during the MLA convention. Through the generous hospitality of

The National Geographic Society, the awards-dinner was held in the lovely new facilities that had just been opened. Honored at the CNL 10th-anniversary awards-dinner were René Wellek, Victor Lange, Vartan Gregorian and Ambassador Robert W. Searby—all of whom had been (and continue to be) instrumental in the expansion of CNL and had proved to be emphatic spokespersons for the ideals and projects of the Council. Presentors were Frank J. Warnke (for René Wellek), Marilyn Gaddis Rose (for Victor Lange), Vahe Oshagan (for Vartan Gregorian), and Henry Paolucci (for Ambassador Searby).

More recently—1985 on—CNL has joined forces with groups such as "Columbus: Countdown 1992" to help promote projects and publications which underscore the multi-ethnic nature of the great celebration scheduled for 1992. CNL/MLA meetings in 1986 and 1987 will feature panels on Columbus; and those presentations will be available in future issues of *CNL/WR*.

Most rewarding, finally, has been the critical reception accorded our *RNL* volumes throughout the world. Reviews have appeared in such places as the *Sunday Times, Cygnus, Littcrit, Osmania Journal of English Studies, Indian Literature, New Quest* (all in India); *Odjek* (Yugoslavia); *Il Veltro* (Rome), *Il corriere della sera, Il resto del carlino, Il messagero* (Italy); *CRNLE, Australian Literary Studies* (Australia); *Dagbladet, Norsk I Utlandet, Scandinavica, The Scandinavian-American Bulletin,* etc. dealing with Norway; *The Armenian Reporter, The Armenian Mirror Spectator, Ararat, The Modern Language Journal, Choice, Sunday Journal and Star, New York Times,* and many other newspapers and journals in Russia, China, Turkey, Europe and USA.

As we enter phase two of our long-range program, we encourage all members and potential contributors to participate in the many activities and projects sponsored by CNL. In this second phase of our long-range programming, we continue to invite contributions for *CNL/WR* as well as ideas and potential presentations for future CNL/MLA or similar panels and discussion groups, and ideas for *RNL* volumes. Most important, we urge all members to consult with their colleagues about joining CNL in a consortium pilot project which will help structure multinational comparative literary studies in a cultural network that will facilitate expanded programs throughout the United States. Such a project does not require large funding; the blueprint is already in place; and the material and human resources are available to us. In the *CNL/WR*s that follow and in our contacts with colleagues both in our formal official presentations and informally through correspondence, we hope to keep exploring the problems that must be resolved in order to launch practical expanded programs in comparative literary studies. Most important: the "continuing dialogue" must not stop nor must it stay locked in preliminary and at this point obvious arguments. New definitions must be articulated; priorities must be established; "cluster" groupings should be worked out, together with all the necessary cultural buttressing; an assessment of material and human resources must be made and utilized in the best possible way; texts must be sorted out and modest translations provided for working purposes, etc.

For now, however, our members both here and abroad should be congratulated for their perseverance and their faith in a project that has proved its worth and an organization that has much to offer in the years ahead.

[The pages that follow contain photographs and summaries of the highlights of the CNL "Retrospective" covering the last 10 years.]

SHAKESPEARE AND ENGLAND

Special Editor: JAMES G. McMANAWAY

Contributors

"Introduction: Thomas Cromwell and the Birth of Shakespeare's England" (*Anne Paolucci*)

"Social Assent and Dissent in Shakespeare's Plays" (*T.J.B. Spencer*)

"Didacticism in Shakespearean Comedy: Renaissance Theory and Practice" (*Kenneth Muir*)

"Racial Terms for Africans in Elizabethan England" (*Eldred Jones*)

"Shakespeare and the Structure of Tudor Society" (*M. C. Bradbrook*)

"Shakespeare's English: The Core Vocabulary" (*Marvin Spevack*)

"Shakespeare and the New Economics of His Time" (*Giorgio Melchiori*)

" 'The True Concord of Well-Tuned Sounds': Shakespeare and Music" (*R. W. Ingram*)

"Shakespeare: Bibliographical Spectrum" (*J. A. Lavin*)

"Review Article: Shakespeare's 'Contemporary Relevance'—From Klein to Kott to Knight" (*Richard C. Clark*)

REVIEW OF NATIONAL LITERATURES

CNL RECEPTION HONORING JAMES G. MCMANAWAY (Editor of the *RNL* volume, *Shakespeare and England.*) Prof. McManaway (left) shown with Dr. Anne Paolucci and Dr. Richard J. Schoeck (Editor of the *RNL* volume, *Canada*.)

Prof. McManaway with Prof. Giovanni Cecchetti (UCLA) and Prof. Vincent Quinn.

Shakespeare Summerfest

"SHAKESPEARE AND THE WORLD"

PROJECT DIRECTOR: Shakespeare Summerfest
Bernard Beckerman, Chairman,
Theatre Arts, Columbia University

DIRECTOR: "Shakespeare and the World"
Anne Paolucci, President,
Council on National Literatures

June 17: Opening Address by TOM STOPPARD.

June 20: "Shakespeare and the Afro-American Community" (opening lecture by Professor Errol Hill). Scene from *Othello*, directed by Darryl Croxton, Artistic Director and Producer (Daragon Productions) with Mercie J. Hinton, Jr., Robert Jackson, Darryl Croxton, Albert Neal, Elizabeth Page, Sundra Jean Williams. Brief informal talk by Earle Hyman: "An Actor's Experience with Shakespeare."

July 11: "Shakespeare in the Hispanic World," the impact of Shakespeare on Hispanic theatre and letters. Introduction: Dr. André Franco (Coordinator/Director), with Raul Davila, David Crommett, Francesco Prado, Elia Enid Cadilla, Soledad Romero.

July 18: "The Greeks Meet the Elizabethan." Introduction: Yannis Simonides (Coordinator/Director), with Anna Makrakis and Isadore Sideris.

July 25: "Shakespeare in Germany": Scenes, Songs, and History. Maurice Edwards (Coordinator/Director), with Annette Becker, Warren Kliewer, Will Taylor, Robert Corman (pianist).

August 1: "Shakespeare in Japan." Introduction and showing of 1957 production of *Throne of Blood.*

August 8: "Shakespeare and the Armenian Theatre." Dr. Nishan Parlakian (Coordinator/Director), with Herand Markarian, Elizabeth Khodabash, Hovhannes Bezdikian, Shoghere Markarian.

August 15: "Shakespeare, Our Contemporary." Lecture by Dr. Anne Paolucci, Director of "Shakespeare and the World" and Associate Director of *Shakespeare Summerfest.*

August 22: "The Hamlet-Myth in Nineteenth-Century France." Dr. Rosette Lamont (Coordinator/Director), with Joanna Adler, Noble Shropshire, David Warrilow.

September 5: "The Many Faces of Love: Shakespeare's Italy." Dr. Ben Termine (Coordinator/Director). Music.

September 12: "Shakespeare in Russia": excerpts from poetry, fiction, and music. Maurice Edwards (Coordinator/Director), with Andrej Kodjak, and others.

September 13: "Shakespeare in the Yiddish Theatre." Wolf Younin (Coordinator/Director), with Mel Gordon, Michael Gorrin and Rita Karin.

September 18: "Shakespeare on the Turkish Stage": an informal talk on "Shakespeare in Ataturk's Turkey," by Tunc Yalman, and selections and reminiscences by Cigdem Selisik-Onat and Shirin Devrim-Trainer.

ISBN: 0-918680-19-0   GHCNL 900/$4.95

Each of the segments was different in the execution, although the planning followed some general guidelines: readings from scenes or portions of scenes in two languages, with an introduction and commentary by the director of each segment—who very often took part in the readings as well. This general blueprint produced such various programs as readings from French poets who were inspired by Hamlet; arias and general historical background about translations and the reception of Shakespeare in Germany, together with readings in English flowing into German and back into English; the Turkish segment, which was a combination of historical backgrounds, readings in two languages prefaced by anecdotes and personal introductions to the dramatic presentations by the actresses; the Hispanic segment, perhaps the longest, but in a way one of the most interesting—for participants and audience a "journey of discovery" in many ways, especially in the impact of Shakespeare on the nation that was, in the playwright's day, England's most bitter enemy; Greek, Yiddish, Russian, Armenian and others—each superbly executed and structured in totally different ways. What became apparent again and again was the emotional impact (more perhaps than the actual lines and language) that determined the stage presentation in each case. It was evident that cultural realities shaped the reception of Shakespeare in different parts of the world, and these nuances came through beautifully in the way the actors delivered their lines, as well as in the very choice of plays.

Prof. Rosette Lamont (Director and participant): "The *Hamlet* Myth in Nineteenth-Century France"

David Warrilow reciting Laforgue's *Hamlet* ("The *Hamlet* Myth in Nineteenth-Century France")

"The Many Faces of Love: Shakespeare's Italy"
(Directed by Ben Termine)

"The Many Faces of Love: Shakespeare's Italy"
(Directed by Ben Termine)

"Shakespeare in the Hispanic World" (Directed by André Franco)

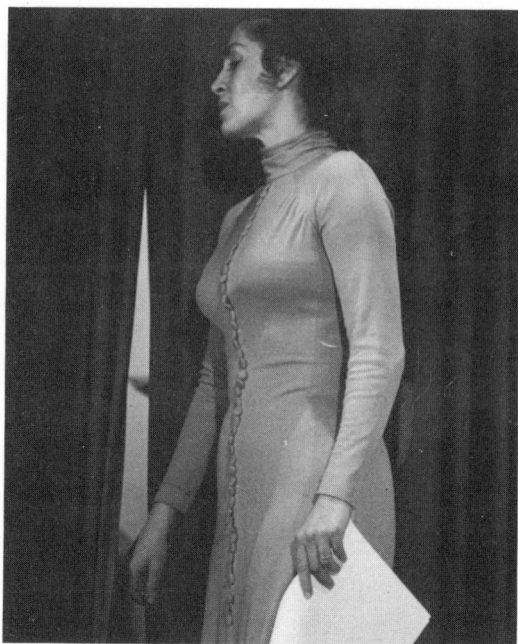

"The Greeks Meet the Elizabethans"

Left to right: Isadore Sideris, Anna Makrakis, Yannis Simonides

Anna Makrakis and Yannis Simonides

"Shakespeare on the Turkish Stage" (Directed by Tunc Halman)

Dr. Anne Paolucci (President CNL and Director of "Shakespeare and the World" delivering the opening lecture for the program: *Shakespeare, Our Contemporary.*

Dr. Anne Paolucci receiving an award for the "Shakespeare and the World" program from Dr. Robert John.

PRESENTATION OF THE *ARMENIA* VOLUME OF *RNL* TO DR. VARTAN GREGORIAN, President and Chief Executive Officer, New York Public Library: Spring, 1984

Dr. Gregorian (shown center in photographs above) was instrumental in getting a substantial grant for the *Armenia* volume of *RNL* (one of the most impressive in the *RNL* series todate). On the left: Dr. Anne Paolucci.

ARMENIA

Special Editor: Vahe Oshagan

ANNE PAOLUCCI
*Armenia's Literary Heritage: National Focus and
Universal Receptiveness*

VAHE OSHAGAN
A Brief Survey of Armenian Literature

ELENA ALEẌANIAN
19th Century Armenian Realism and Its International Relations

JAMES ETMEKJIAN
*Western European and Modern Armenian Literary
Relations up to 1915*

VARAK NERSISSIAN
Medieval Armenian Poetry and Its Relation to Other Literatures

BOGHOS LEVON ZEKIYAN
*Personal Tragedy and Cultural Backgrounds in the
Poetry of Bedros Tourian*

HRAND TAMRAZIAN
Yeghishe Charentz and the Socialist Revolution

LEVON HAKHVERDIAN
Armenian Classical Drama and Its International Context

VAHE OSHAGAN
Cosmopolitanism in West Armenian Literature

VREJ NERSESSIAN
Bibliographical Spectrum on Modern Armenian Literature

NISHAN PARLAKIAN / HENRY PAOLUCCI
Review Article: Armenian Literature Between East and West

TENTH ANNIVERSARY AWARDS-DINNER, December 28, 1984, National Geographic Society, Washington D.C.

The elegant 10th-anniversary awards dinner was attended by a number of CNL contributing editors and *RNL* special editors—including John J. Deeney (The Chinese University of Hong Kong), Dr. Marilyn Gaddis Rose (SUNY Binghamton), Dr. Frank J. Warnke (U. of Georgia/Athens), Dr. Eniko Basa (Library of Congress), Dr. Vahe Oshagan, Dr. Ron Docksai (Assistant Secretary for Legislation, Department of Health and Human Services), Dr. Frank Bonora (National Italian American Foundation), Dr. Thomas Greene (Yale), Dr. Elizabeth W. Trahan (The Monterey Institute for International Studies), Dr. Jean-Pierre Barricelli (U of California/Riverside), Dr. Victor Lange (Princeton), Dr. Maristella Lorch (Director, Center for Italian Studies, Columbia U), Dr. A. Owen Aldridge, Dr. Calvin Linton, Dr. Rosette Lamont (Graduate Center CUNY), Dr. Charles Burton Marshall (former Special Aide to Dean Acheson), Ms. Susan Carlin (Director, Public Affairs, Armenian Assembly of America), Dr. Philip A. Fulvi (Vice-President and Assistant Editor, The Pirandello Society of America), Dr. Nishan Parlakian (Director of Armenian segment of "Shakespeare and the World"), and many other prominent Washington personalities and academics from the United States and abroad.

The official "presentations" as published in the evening's program. are given below.

Dr. Anne Paolucci (President, CNL) welcoming guests to the 10th-anniversary awards dinner.

66

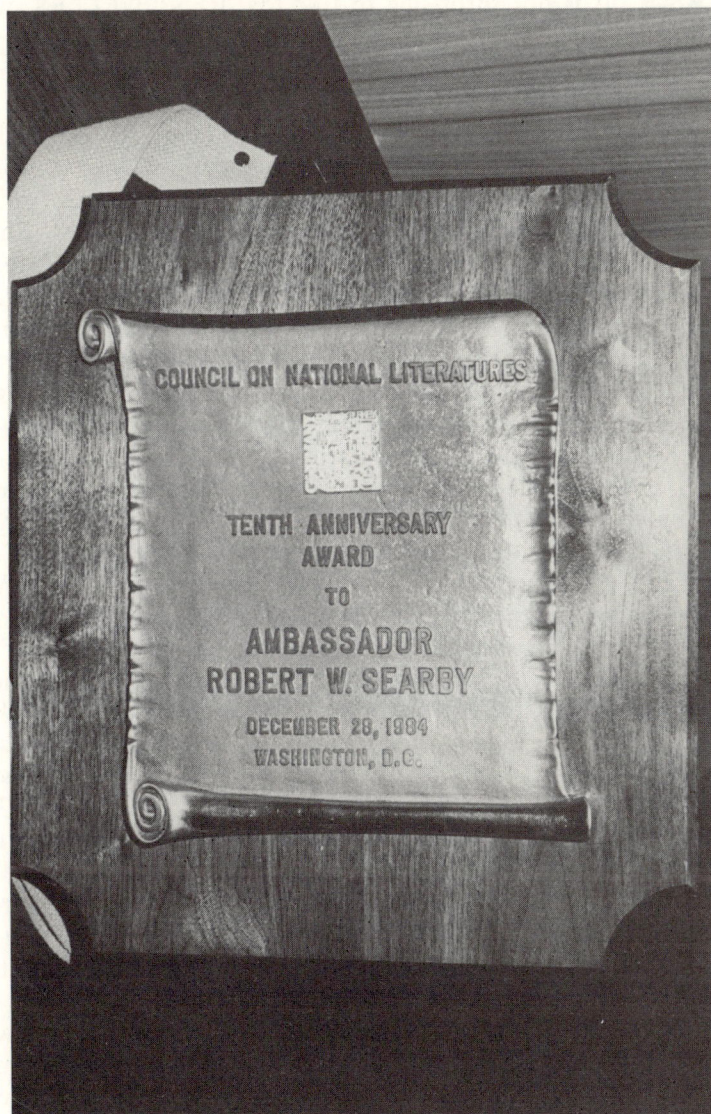

The bronze plaque designed for the 10th-anniversary awards.

It is not surprising to find that RENÉ WELLEK, without question the leading comparatist of our time, has a European background which includes a university degree in Prague, honorary degrees from Lawrence College, Oxford University, Harvard, the University of Rome, the University of Maryland, Boston College, Columbia, University of Munich, University of East Anglia, University of Montreal, University of Louvain—to name a few. His teaching experience is no less impressive in its variety: Princeton, Smith, Prague again, London University, Iowa, Yale—where he was Sterling Professor in Comparative Literature, and later Sterling Emeritus Professor in Comparative Literature. But perhaps the most important aspect of Dr. Wellek's career is in the variety of the subjects and areas he has covered and particularly his efforts to provide—as early as the 1940s—the guidelines and important priorities that have in fact shaped the development of comparative literary studies both in this country and abroad. A recipient of many important academic awards, including Guggenheim fellowships, Fulbright fellowships, the Distinguished Scholar Humanities Award of the American Council of Learned Societies, the Bollingen Foundation Award, Mary Peabody Waite Award, and fellowships of the National Endowment the Humanities, Dr. Wellek has also served on the boards of the leading associations in our discipline: President of the International Comparative Literature Association, Vice-President and later President of the Modern Language Association, President of the Czech Society of Arts and Science in the US, President of the Modern Humanities Research Association. His THEORY OF LITERATURE, jointly authored with Austin Warren (and available now in at least 22 languages, besides English), is perhaps his best known work, and is still a classic text for all comparatists. But there is much more to the achievement of Rene Wellek in literary theory and criticism. We all rejoice that the monumental two-volume Festschrift of that title, LITERARY THEORY AND CRITICISM (Peter Lang, Bern & NY, 1984), edited by Joseph P. Strelka, has now appeared. This work of nearly 1500 pages (including an invaluable bibliography) is indeed —as Henri Peyre has said—"a striking tribute not only to Rene Wellek himself but also to the American achievement in the realms of literary theory, criticism, general and comparative literature," an achievement that has worked toward "the mutual understanding of cultures." In its statement of purpose, which appears on the first page of every volume of CNL's series REVIEW OF NATIONAL LITERATURES, Professor Wellek is quoted for his lucid reminder that international studies need firm and careful structuring and constant monitoring if the discipline is to avoid "an indiscriminate smattering, a vague sentimental cosmopolitanism" that often mistakes the poverty of national literatures for their wealth. He remarks correctly that in the comparative study of what is sometimes called world literature, it is "the problem of 'nationality' and of the distinct contributions of the individual nations to this general literary process which should be realized as central."

VARTAN GREGORIAN

President and Chief Executive Officer of The New York Public Library since June 1981, VARTAN GREGORIAN has used the past three years to greatly expand the Library's role as a center of culture and learning, while at the same time raising the number of annual donors and the total of private support funding for the central library and its 82 branches to the highest level in the institution's history. This has been a truly staggering accomplishment for a scholar, award-winning teacher, writer, linguist who had previously pursued a distinguished academic career at the University of Pennsylvania, serving as Dean of the Faculty of Arts and Sciences (1974-1978) and as Provost of the University (1978-1980), while continuing to occupy an endowed professorial chair in Armenian and Caucasian history from 1972 to 1984. His previous teaching had been at San Francisco State University, UCLA, and the University of Texas at Austin. Dr. Gregorian has been the recipient of numeous awards, including the Danforth Foundation's E. H. Harbison Distinguished Teaching Award, fellowships from the American Council of Learned Societies, the Guggenheim Foundation, the American Philosophical Society, the Ford Foundation and many others. He received his doctorate in history and humanities in 1964 (and his B.A. in 1958) from Stanford University, where he was elected to Phi Beta Kappa. The recipient of many honorary degrees (Brown, Franklin & Marshall, Drew, Boston, Jewish Theological Seminary), Dr. Gregorian serves on the National Advisory Board of the College of Arts and Sciences of Northwestern University, the Board of Visitors of the Graduate School and University Center of City University of New York (chairman), the Library Advisory Council of Johns Hopkins, and the Advisory Council of the Center for Publishing at New York University. An Armenian born in Iran, Dr. Gregorian is the author of THE EMERGENCE OF MODERN AFGHANISTAN: POLITICS OF REFORM AND MODERNIZATION (considered the definitive work in its field), and has written and lectured extensively on Armenian culture and history, ethnicity, minorities, the Soviet Union, the challenges of contemporary culture, the future of learning, problems of higher education and literacy. Recently, Dr. Gregorian was influential in getting significant support for CNL's volume on ARMENIA and in November, at a presentation-reception held in The New York Public Library, he received the first copies (paperback and hardbound) of this extraordinary volume from CNL President Dr. Anne Paolucci, who noted that it was one of the most important in the RNL series "since it focuses on a literature that is in every way a national cultural expression much like that of the Jews—who, long before Israel came into being in our time, cultivated and cherished their cultural heritage with ardor."

ROBERT W. SEARBY

Quite in the spirit of the Council on National Literatures' statement of purpose—which he helped to formulate—AMBASSADOR ROBERT W. SEARBY brings to our international relations a sense of appreciation for the national identities and cultural achievements of the world's diverse peoples which is as remarkably profound as it is unassuming. As Deputy Under Secretary for International Affairs in the United States Department of Labor since 1981, and increasingly since his appointments as chairman of the U.S. delegations to the Geneva conferences of the ·International Labor Organization in 1982 and as Special Ambassador early in 1984, Ambassador Searby has impressed his counterparts in other governments with his keen awareness of the importance of the world's diverse literatures as expressions of national character and as repositories of national cultures in their most vital and most readily communicable forms. After receiving his B.A. in history at Iona College, Ambassador Searby served with the Army's 101st Airborne Division in Vietnam, where he put to use his specialized study in Mandarin Chinese and related Southeast Asian languages. After resuming his studies for an M.A. in St. John's University and a doctorate in political philosophy and international relations at Fordham, he taught briefly at St. John's and the New York Institute of Technology, where he became Academic Coordinator of the Institute's Criminal Justice Programs. During this period he performed invaluable services, also, as Executive Director of The Walter Bagehot Research Council and was on the editorial staff of the Council on National Literatures. While still in New York, Ambassador Searby served as the Executive Director of the New York State Committee for Jobs and Energy Independence (co-chaired by former Secretary of Labor,

Peter J. Brennan and Charles Luce, President of Con Edison). His skills as a labor-management arbitrator; his manifest talents in resolving issues of immigration, codes of international employment, technology transfer and trade agreements; and his many articles and lectures on varieties of diplomatic recognition, arms control, human rights policies, the Polish and Arab-Israeli crises, all reflect the principles of global understanding that serve as guidelines for CNL—principles which Ambassador Searby has shown to be compatible with the highest aims of American international diplomacy.

VICTOR LANGE

A native of Leipzig, Germany, VICTOR LANGE studied at Oxford, the Sorbonne, Munich, and the University of Toronto before returning to Leipzig for his Ph.D.. One of the most sought-after lecturers in his field, Dr. Lange has taught primarily at the Universities of Toronto, Cornell, and Princeton—where he was chairman of the Department of German and John N. Woodhull Professor of Modern Languages, and where he has been Professor Emeritus since 1977. He has been an honored scholar and guest professor at universities and centers of learning throughout the U.S. and around the world, including the Free University of Berlin, the University of Chicago, the University of California (Berkeley, Davis, La Jolla), Heidelberg, Cologne, Columbia, Michigan, Munich, Auckland, The Australian National University, Melbourne, Yale, NYU, Pennsylvania, and the Graduate Center of CUNY. He has been a ranking officer in the Modern Language Association, the American Comparative Literature Association, the International Association of Germanic Studies, the American Society of Eighteenth Century Studies, and university chapters of Phi Beta Kappa, as well as Director of the American Council of German Studies and a Trustee of Goethe House in New York. A recipient of Guggenheim, Fulbright, and NEH fellowships, Professor Lange is best known for his works in modern German literature, Goethe's fiction, Schlegel's literary theory, German Expressionism, contemporary German poetry, Thomas Mann, and aesthetic and literary theory. In 1978 he prepared, as special editor, the RNL volume on GERMAN EXPRESSIONISM—for which he also wrote one of the leading articles. He was honored by the Federal Republic of Germany in 1959 with the Grosses Bundesverdienstkreuz and in 1967 received the Gold Goethe Medal of the Goethe Institute of Munich. Dr. Lange's services on the Executive Board of CNL have always been most generously offered and greatly appreciated.

Dr. René Wellek receiving the CNL award from Dr. Anne Paolucci
(President, CNL) and Dr. Frank J. Warnke (Presentor).

Dr. and Mrs. René Wellek.

Dr. Rosette Lamont, Dr. Anne Paolucci, Dr. Wellek, Mrs. Wellek.

Dr. Vartan Gregorian, President and Chief Executive Office,
New York Public Library, receiving the CNL award from Dr. Anne
Paolucci and Dr. Vahe Oshagan (Presentor).

Dr. Gregorian and Dr. Maristella Lorch.

Dr. Gregorian and guests.

Ambassador Robert W. Searby (Deputy Undersecretary for International Affairs, Department of Labor) receiving the CNL award from Dr. Anne Paolucci and Dr. Henry Paolucci (Presentor).

Ambassador Searby with guests and Mrs. Searby (far right).

Dr. Victor Lange receiving the CNL award from Dr. Anne Paolucci and Dr. Marilyn Gaddis Rose (Presentor).

Dr. and Mrs. Victor Lange.

Dr. Victor Lange and Dr. René Wellek.

Among the guests: Dr. Ron Docksai, Assistant Secretary for Legislation, Department of Health and Human Services, with Dr. Henry Paolucci (Special Coordinator for CNL) and Mrs. Docksai.

Among the guests: Dr. Philip A. Fulvi, Vice President, The Pirandello Society of America and member of the International Academic Committee (representing France) of "Columbus: Countdown 1992" (center), with Mrs. Fulvi (third from left) and Dr. Frank D. Grande, President of Griffon House Publications (third from right).

Dr. Frank D. Grande delivers the closing remarks at the CNL dinner.

Review of National Literatures

REVIEW OF NATIONAL LITERATURES is a forum for scholars and critics concerned with literature as the expression of national character and as the repository of national culture in its most vital and most readily communicable form. The editors recognize the validity of the critical perspective of recent decades when, as a corrective against the excesses of an exclusively nationalist orientation, it has seemed important to emphasize internationalist and even anti-nationalist tendencies in the study of literature. But they also recognize the validity of Professor René Wellek's strictures against deliberate cultivation of an internationalist point of view which has the effect, as he says, of encouraging "an indiscriminate smattering, a vague, sentimental cosmopolitanism" that often mistakes the poverty of national literatures for their wealth. Professor Wellek has remarked correctly that in the comparative study of what is sometimes called world literature, it is "the problem of 'nationality' and of the distinct contributions of the individual nations to this general literary process which should be realized as central."

On the assumption so ably expressed by a distinguished statesman of the 20th century that "it would be reactionary to abolish those distinctions of language, literature, and art, which give to the human mind its infinite variety," REVIEW OF NATIONAL LITERATURES undertakes to encourage a continuing reassessment of the wealth of national literatures—from the earliest to the most recent— as a prerequisite for the understanding and diffusion of "world literature" in its profoundest sense.

Each issue focuses on a national culture, or, more particularly, on a representative theme, author, literary movement, or critical tendency. in an effort to provide substantial and concentrated materials for comparative study. To insure competent presentation of highly specialized or novel topics—such as contemporary literary developments in a new or emerging nation—the regular editors enlist, when necessary, the collaboration of "special editors."

Review of National Literatures

EDITOR: ANNE PAOLUCCI

STILL AVAILABLE . . . . . .

[SEMI-ANNUAL SERIES: 1970 – 1975*]

MACHIAVELLI '500
HEGEL IN COMPARATIVE LITERATURE *(Sp. Ed. Frederick G. Weiss)*
IRAN *(Sp. Ed. Javad Haidari)*
BLACK AFRICA *(Sp. Ed. Albert S. Gerard)*
RUSSIA: THE SPIRIT OF NATIONALISM *(Sp. Ed. Charles A. Moser)*
SHAKESPEARE AND ENGLAND *(Sp. Ed. James G. McManaway)*
TURKEY: FROM EMPIRE TO NATION *(Sp. Ed. Talat Sait Halman)*
THE FRANCE OF CLAUDEL *(Sp. Ed. Henri Peyre)*
THE MULTINATIONAL LITERATURE OF YUGOSLAVIA *(Sp. Ed. Albert B. Lord)*
GREECE: THE MODERN VOICE *(Sp. Ed. Peter Mackridge)*
CHINA'S LITERARY IMAGE* *(Sp. Ed. Paul K. T. Sih)*

[NEW A N N U A L SERIES: 1976 –]

CANADA *(Sp. Ed. Richard J. Schoeck)*
HOLLAND *(Sp. Ed. Frank J. Warnke)*
GERMAN EXPRESSIONISM *(Sp. Ed. Victor Lange)*
INDIA *(Sp. Ed. Ronald Warwick)*
AUSTRALIA *(Sp. Ed. L. A. C. Dobrez)*
NORWAY *(Sp. Ed. Sverre Lyngstad)*
ARMENIA** *(Sp. Ed. Vahe Oshagan)*
PIRANDELLO *(Sp. Ed. Anne Paolucci)*
COLUMBUS*** *(Sp. Ed. Henry Paolucci)*
JAPAN*** *(Sp. Ed. John Gillespie)*
COMPARATIVE LITERARY THEORY: AN OVERVIEW*** *(Sp. Ed. Anne Paolucci)*
HUNGARY*** *(Sp. Ed. Moses M. Nagy)*

Only one volume issued in 1975.
**Hardbound volume also available for $40.*
*** *In preparation.*

ALL VOLUMES: $23 each; $US ONLY, PREPAID (P/H incl.)
TO ORDER: Send check and titles to CNL, P. O. Box 81
Whitestone, New York 11357.